Financial Secrets to Franchising Success

A Guide to Creditor Protection,
Tax Reduction and Financial Freedom

Christopher R. Jarvis, MBA
Glenn M. Terrones, Esq.
David B. Mandell, JD, MBA
Danielle C. Jarvis, Esq.

Library of Congress Cataloging-in-Publication Data:
Jarvis, Christopher, 1970–
    Financial Secrets to Franchising Success: A Guide to Creditor Protection, Tax Reduction and Financial Freedom / by Christopher Jarvis, Glenn M. Terrones, David B. Mandell, Danielle C. Jarvis.
        p. cm.
    Includes bibliographical references and index.
    ISBN 1-890415-20-0
    1. Executions (Law)—United States. 2. Debtor and creditors—United States 3. Estate planning—United States. 4. Tax planning—United States I. Mandell, David B., 1968– II. Title.

Book cover & interior designed by Rebecca Krzyzaniak
cover image: www.freeimages.co.uk

Printed in the United States of America

10 9 8 7 6 5 4 3 2 1

This book is a result of our experience and research as well as the knowledge and expertise of dozens of professionals across the country. Without our "team" of experts, we would not be able to bring up-to-date information and cutting edge strategies to our high-net-worth and high income clients.

We would like to thank all of those individuals who have helped us decipher the information sent to us by clients, identify areas of concern or need, create specialized programs and enhance existing ones — all within the guidelines of state and federal statutes.

We would like to thank all of the professionals who have contributed greatly to this book and to our overall operations across the country. A partial list includes, but is not limited to:

Celia R. Clark, Dale Edwards, Dr. Arnold Goldstein, Alan Brown, David Wright, Christine Terrones, Ajay Keshap, Renee Cardriche, Danny Wexler, Vito Lanuti, and the others we apologize for accidentally omitting.

We would like to offer a special thanks to all the members of the Wealth Protection Alliance who are so valuable in the implementation of the strategies we recommend. Without their assistance, clients around the country would not receive the valuable planning they desire.

A list of the firms and individuals in the WPA can be found in the Appendix.

Christopher R. Jarvis

Christopher is a financial planner and co-founder of Jarvis & Mandell Consulting and the Wealth Protection Alliance. He is the author of a number of books, including *Wealth Protection: Build and Preserve Your Financial Fortress©*. Mr. Jarvis has been quoted in the Wall Street Journal and the Los Angeles Business Journal. He has appeared on Bloomberg Television and over 100 radio stations. Chris has been published in *The Detroit Free Press, Orange Country Register, Female Entrepreneur, MXB, Yachts International,* and *InFlight*. He has lectured at the International College of Surgeons, Association of Chamber of Commerce Executives, and New York Chapter of Financial Planning Association (NY FPA). Mr. Jarvis holds an honor's degree in applied mathematics from the University of Rhode Island. He earned a Master's of Business Administration from UCLA. Chris was awarded the LA Chapter of the Young President's Organization's (YPO) Ken Kennedy Fellowship for his entrepreneurial achievement.

Glenn M. Terrones

Glenn is an asset protection and estate planning attorney in California. Mr. Terrones is the author of several articles on the topics of asset protection and estate planning that have appeared in such periodicals as *Yachts International, Verdict,* and *Hispanic Business Review*. He is a co-author of *Wealth Protection, MD: the Ultimate Financial Guide for 21st Century Physicians©*. Mr. Terrones has specific expertise working with physicians and franchise owners. He was a judicial extern for the 9th Circuit of Court of Appeals. Glenn has been the key legal speaker at the annual meeting of the International College of Surgeons. Mr. Terrones graduated Cum Laude from the University of Pennsylvania and earned his law degree from the Boalt Hall School of Law at the University of California.

David B. Mandell, JD, MBA

David Mandell is an attorney, author, and authority in the fields of risk management, asset protection, tax, and financial planning. He serves as an attorney in the Law Offices of David B. Mandell, P.C. in New York, a principal of Jarvis & Mandell Consulting and also co-founder of The Wealth Protection Alliance. As a writer, Mr. Mandell has co-authored the book *Wealth Protection: Build & Preserve Your Financial Fortress*© (Wiley 2003), *Wealth Protection, MD*© and *Risk Management for the Practicing Physician*©. David has been interviewed as an expert in such national media as Bloomberg and FOX-TV and is a member of the California and New York Bar Associations.

Danielle C. Jarvis, Esq.

Danielle Jarvis is an attorney and financial professional with licenses in insurance and securities. Mrs. Jarvis has served as general counsel of a broker-dealer and has experience as an estate planning and corporate attorney in Nebraska. Mrs. Jarvis has extensive experience working with farmers and ranchers. Danielle attended Creighton University where she earned an honor's degree in English. Mrs. Jarvis earned her law degree from Creighton University's School of Law. She is a member of the Nebraska Bar Association.

Why We Wrote This Book

As authors of five books and over 100 asset protection articles, as columnists in many of the nation's leading medical magazines, and as advisors to hundreds of professionals and business owners, we have our finger on the pulse of the American businessman's mindset. More specifically, we know what the current lawsuit crisis is doing to many of you. It's making you frustrated, financially stressed, and — in some cases — forcing you to consider giving up the operation of your business completely.

In speaking with thousands of businessmen like you over the years, we invariably hear the same question: "What can we do about this?" In order to help business owners like you handle this burgeoning problem, we decided to create this book. This book is a combination of a number of things, including: excerpts from our last book, *Wealth Protection, M.D.* (Guardian Publishing (800) 554-7233), Jarvis and Mandell's previous book, *Wealth Protection: Build and Preserve Your Financial Fortress* (available at **www.mywealthprotection.com**), conversations with our clients and colleagues, articles we have written, and, of course, recent developments in the law.

If you are a business owner who owns restaurant franchises, car dealerships, real estate developments, farms, or any other business that might have multiple locations, you should think of yourself as a franchise owner. If you think of yourself as a franchise owner and you want to get the most out of your businesses and want to limit your lawsuit risks and your tax liabilities, you need to read the rest of this book!

We Are Practical, Not Political

We are financial and legal advisors to doctors, franchise owners, real estate investors and businessmen. We are not policymakers or politicians. In this book, we will not discuss how the laws regarding non-economic damages in tort cases should be limited. We will not opine on the fiscal policies of the insurance carriers or the attitudes of trial lawyers. These elements, and changes to them, are beyond your direct control. While rallying with your colleagues into a political group may be effective for the long-term, we will let other voices (like your local business association or chamber of commerce) take up that cry.

Instead, our focus here — as it is with our clients — is to show you *what you can do to improve your personal situation in this burgeoning crisis even if political relief never comes to fruition.* Specifically, we will show you:

1. How to structure your franchise operations to minimize creditor risks and promote financial flexibility and efficiency.
2. How to structure your personal assets to minimize creditor risks and reduce unnecessary taxes.
3. How to integrate your business and personal planning to help you achieve the financial freedom you desire.

Before we delve into the strategies that have benefited savvy business owners, we must review some wealth protection concepts and misconceptions so we can have a strong foundation. Upon this foundation, we hope to help you build your financial fortress.

It is our hope that this book helps answer many of your questions and, more importantly, shows you what assets you need to protect and how you can protect them. If, after reading this book, you still have questions, please feel free to contact us via phone or e-mail. We are happy to assist clients in all 50 states in person in our offices, over the phone, or in person through one of our 60 satellite offices (all part of the prestigious Wealth Protection Alliance, **wealthprotectionalliance. com**). For more information on working with us, please contact any of the authors to arrange a meeting.

Jarvis & Mandell Consulting, LLC

2321 Rosecrans Avenue, Suite 1280
El Segundo, California 90245
(310) 536-0700
jarvis@jarvisandmandell.com

Law Offices of David. B. Mandell, P.C.

100 Park Avenue, 33rd Floor
New York, New York 10017
(212) 972-1222
dmandell@mandellpc.com

Law Offices of Glenn M. Terrones, P.C.

2321 Rosecrans Avenue, Suite 1280
El Segundo, California 90245
(310) 536-8411
terrones@jarvisandmandell.com

If you would prefer to arrange a meeting with one of our Wealth Protection Alliance offices in your area, please contact Todd Goldfarb at (800) 554-7233 or via email at goldfarb@ wealthprotectionalliance.com.

CHAPTER ONE

The Severity of the Crisis at Hand

Every business owner is at risk to a variety of lawsuits. These threats range from employee risks and product liability to personal lawsuits and premises liability. Employee risks include sexual harassment, wrongful termination, discrimination (race, age, gender or sexual preference) and others. Product liability includes any liability that arises from anything you sell to a customer. This could be a toy that is swallowed by a child to a faulty machine part to a building that has mold or mildew. Personal lawsuits include accidents that take place while driving company vehicles as well as libel and slander or assault and battery by you OR by any of your employees. Basically anything that takes place because of an action of one of your employees can result in liability to you. Perhaps more troubling is that anything that happens on your property can result in a lawsuit against you. These risks would fall into the category of premises liability.

Recent studies and case decisions in the area of premises liability are, without question, cause for alarm. According to the National Safety Council, there are approximately 9 million disabling slip and fall injuries each year.[1] Each day, 25,000 slip and fall accidents require medical attention.[2] Over 540,000 slip-and-fall injuries result in hospitalization of the claimant and over 20,000 result in a fatality in North America each year.[3]

More than 1 million restaurant guests are injured in slip-and-fall accidents each year and it is estimated that the food service industry spends more than $2 billion each year for such injuries.[4] Perhaps more astonishing is the fact that the amount spent on slip-and-fall claims has been rising by nearly 10% per year.[5] Small restaurants — those with fewer than 20 workers — make up 72% of the 7,400 registered employers in the restaurant industry and they generate nearly 40% of the compensation claim costs of the overall restaurant industry.[6]

Consider the following amazing events that have occurred within our legal system in the last few years:

- A jury in New Mexico awarded Stella Liebeck $2,900,000 in her lawsuit against McDonald's for damages alleged to have occurred after spilling coffee on herself that was "too hot."

- A California man is awarded $5,400,000 in a successful lawsuit against Costco for injuries he sustained when he was struck by someone else's car in the parking lot.

- A customer in a Bar and Grill is beaten by two patrons and is awarded $3,600,000 in damages by a California jury. The judgment was against the restaurant owner who wasn't even present at the time of the fight!

- A man is killed by inebriated minors while eating in a café and the jury awards the deceased man's family $1,999,999 in a suit against the café owner.

- And, in a case that has not yet occurred (but you know it's coming), an overweight person wins an award of millions against a fast-food franchise by alleging the fast-food franchise is at fault for his or her obesity.

Unfortunately, the liability risk is not limited to premises liability actions. Like any other business owner, you are also at risk for suits alleging wrongful termination, sexual harassment and discrimination. Consider the following:

- A California woman sues her employer, alleging that she was pressured to have sex with a company VP and is awarded $3,000,000;

- A 25-year employee claimed she was wrongfully terminated because of a medical condition and is awarded $19,000,000; and,

- Finally, an employee alleges that his employer wrongfully terminated him in order to avoid payment of a performance bonus and is awarded $2,900,000 (the performance bonus that was lost was a very small percentage of the damages awarded).

What makes these types of cases even more frightening is that your existing liability policies do not cover these types of risks. This means that your only recourse to satisfy this type of judgment is liquidation or attachment of your personal and/or business assets — a scenario that is likely to result in financial ruin.

Even in the case of traditional insurance coverages, liability insurers have indicated that they are losing money and must therefore raise the premium rates of their policyholders. Despite the premium increases, however, losses and expenses for insurers continue to mount and it is likely that this trend will continue.

Does anything we mentioned in the last two pages sound familiar or frighten you? If you are scared, then you should be motivated to do whatever you can to protect yourself and your family. To help you figure out what to do next, we recommend you read this book and take a lot of notes, highlight a number of pages, and start writing down a number of viable alternatives. At the end of the book (Chapter 11), we will explain what to do once you have identified all of your risks and explored a few possible strategies that may help you meet your planning needs.

FOOTNOTES

[1] "The Law & Statistics," by DWG Safe Floors, Inc. (2004-2005, citing statistical data of the National Safety Council)

[2] *Id.*

[3] "Dramatic Slip-Fall Statistics," by Anti-slip Alberta (2001)

[4] "The NFSI Best Practices Project," by the National Floor Study Institute (2003)

[5] *Id.*

[6] "Media Fact Sheet: WCB Restaurant Statistics 1995-1999," by Worksafe BC (February 13, 2001)

CHAPTER TWO

Avoiding Franchise Failure

Do you run your own restaurant or hope to run your own restaurant? Do you own a car dealership? Do you own rental real estate or another type of business that you hope will someday have multiple locations? If your answer to any of these questions is "yes," then you need to consider yourself a "franchisee." If you are trying to "franchise" or replicate some business in multiple locations, then you have double or triple the risks that threaten a business owner who only has one location.

We assume that you want to get the most, financially-speaking, out of your business. To accomplish this goal, you will need to do more than the typical cookie-cutter planning that many accountants and attorneys recommend. Building a franchise business is very similar to building a home. The key to building a successful franchise business is to start with a strong foundation. With a strong structural foundation, you can build the franchise empire you desire without complications. As your franchise business grows, the more pressure that will be placed on the foundation. The more pressure on a faulty foundation, the more likely you are to suffer from a small mistake.

Would you believe us if we told you that most business owners who call us have franchises that are structured with three (3) things in common:

1. Maximum Lawsuit Exposure
2. Minimum Tax Saving Potential
3. Minimum Flexibility

If you think we are kidding, let's take a little quiz and see how you fare:

1. Is the real estate from which you operate your franchise owned or leased by your franchise, the owners of the franchise, or the spouses of the owners of the franchise?

2. Is the equipment in your restaurants(s) owned by your franchise, the owners, or their spouses?

3. Is the franchise agreement authorizing you to operate your franchise in the name of your franchise or in your personal name?

4. If you have more than one (1) franchise, are all of the franchises owned by your lone corporation or by you or your spouse?

5. If there are other owners involved in your franchise business, are you operating your franchise as a general partnership?

6. Do you employ workers through the same company that owns the franchise agreement, real estate, or equipment?

If you said "Yes" to ANY of the six questions above, then your franchise is built on a faulty foundation. The good news is that this book will explain all six of these problems and, more importantly, offer you simple alternative strategies so you're not unnecessarily at risk to any of the problems discussed at the beginning of this chapter.

Franchise Assets Are Typically Owned by the Franchise or by the Owners of the Franchise

Note: In many of these examples and descriptions, we may refer to restaurants, stores or franchises. You can basically consider them to be interchangable throughout. One of the most common asset protection mistakes that restaurant owners make is that the physical assets of the business, such as land or equipment, are usually owned by the restaurant (or corporation operating the restaurant) or by the owners personally. Ownership in this manner places all of the restaurant's assets at risk in the event of a lawsuit — an unnecessary and unacceptable risk. As will be explained further in this book, it is far wiser to have any real estate, leaseholds, franchise agreements, and equipment owned by separate Limited Liability Company(s)

("LLC") and then have your restaurant operation lease (or sublease) the equipment and land from the LLC(s).

Don't worry if you don't know what a limited liability company (LLC) is. We will discuss this entity in detail later in the book. Furthermore, our books (order form is Appendix C) discuss many legal and financial structures and strategies in greater detail.

Multiple Stores Are Owned by One Entity or as a Sole Proprietorship

A second common error in the structure of restaurant operations is that many of you own and operate more than one restaurant but have all of your restaurants owned by one singular corporation or other such entity. In some really unfortunate cases, multiple restaurants are owned as a sole proprietorship (meaning in your own name, in the name of living or family trust or held jointly with a spouse). In either case, you have placed all — that's right — *all* of your restaurants at risk even though liability may arise, or has arisen, in *only one of your stores*. This too is an unacceptable and unnecessary risk. It is far wiser that each of your stores is owned and operated by a separate entity — preferably an LLC or Limited Partnership. This way, if liability arises from the operation of one (1) store, the assets of that particular store are the only assets at risk to that particular claim. The assets of the other stores will not be at risk and the other stores continue operating without any risk of exposure.

The purpose of this book is to help franchise owners identify risks to their franchise business and to their family's financial situation. By addressing the two significant problems mentioned above, and the numerous issues discussed throughout the chapters of this book, you can avoid the most common fatal business mistakes. If you want to ensure that your franchise does not become a failed business, please take many notes as you read the remainder of this book and then be sure to act (Chapter 11 – Next Steps) by working with a Wealth Protection Alliance office in your area.

CHAPTER THREE

Common Asset Protection Myths

Nearly every business training course focuses on helping business owners increase revenues or reduce operational expenses. All of these programs are designed to help you increase profit margins. Of course, we all strive to have wildly successful businesses. However, we must ask "What good is profit if you lose it all to taxes or to lawsuits?"

None of us want to lose our hard-earned wealth to lawsuits. The first step in protecting our wealth from lawsuits is to determine which assets ARE protected and which assets ARE NOT protected. Once we identify which assets are not protected, we can put together a plan to better protect our wealth. Let's begin by dispelling some myths that unfortunate franchise owners believed would benefit them before they learned the truth the hard way and had to start all over again.

You may feel for many reasons that your wealth is safe and that you do not need asset protection. We claim this attitude is naive. Unfortunately, many business owners (especially franchise owners) falsely believe many of the following myths:

Myth #1: "I can't get sued. I'm too careful."

While you need not do anything wrong to find yourself on the wrong end of a lawsuit, there are those who tell us, "I have never been sued before and I can't visualize why I would be sued now."

One woman who attended one of our seminars gave us the same argument as she explained her apathy for asset protection: "I'm a schoolteacher. What legal problems can a schoolteacher have?" True, she may never be sued as a schoolteacher, yet this woman was sued for over one million dollars about a year later for negligently handling her mother's estate.

There are many ways one can be sued today. A lawsuit need not relate directly to your role as a business owner. You may be cautious and careful and still get sued. It is not only doctors, real estate developers, or business owners who incur liability or attract lawsuits; everyone is a potential target.

Certainly, any person who runs a business, has employees, or has repeated contact with the public is not safe. Whenever anything bad happens, plaintiffs "let their fingers do the walking" in the Yellow Pages in an attempt to find a lawyer ready and willing to take the case. Others are also high on the lawsuit hit list: parents of teenage drivers; commercial real estate owners; small business owners; accountants and other business advisors; architects and engineers; corporate officers and directors; directors of charitable organizations; police officers; celebrities; sports figures, and the conspicuously wealthy. It's not what you do, but how much you own that determines your vulnerability.

Myth #2: "I don't need asset protection. I don't have any assets to protect."

This is perhaps the most common misconception about asset protection. It isn't that people without assets need asset protection, but that people have no idea what assets they own and how much risk they face on a daily basis.

The big question to ask yourself is "How would you feel if you lost what few assets you did own?" If your entire wealth consists of just a used car worth $15,000 and $20,000 in equity in your home, how would you feel if tomorrow someone seized your car and home?

If you have any assets you wouldn't want to lose, then you must consider asset protection. Our experience in helping clients with asset protection concerns as part of their comprehensive wealth protection planning has taught us that wealth is relative. It is not only the rich and affluent who need asset protection.

The differences we witness in quality of life during retirement for clients who had similar earnings during their working years are directly related to the mistakes they avoided. Business owners who were not wiped out by taxes, a messy divorce, or any lawsuits typically had far more enjoyable retirements than those clients who made mistakes in the past and were not protected against the financial repercussions that followed. If you want to enjoy the fruits of your labor, now and in retirement, you should take asset protection planning very seriously.

Myth #3: "I don't need protection. I'm insured."

This is another fallacy. You buy a liability policy and figure, "That's it, I'm covered. If I'm sued, my insurance will take care of it."

We can give you many reasons why liability insurance is not a substitute for asset protection. In fact, liability insurance covers only about one in three lawsuits. What do you do about the two out of three lawsuits that will not be covered by insurance? Consider the possibilities: you could get sued for breach of contract, a defaulted loan, or on a family dispute. You could be sued by an employee for wrongful termination, sexual harassment, discrimination or other uninsured acts. How many uninsured claims can be levied against you? The possibilities are endless.

Take a lesson from a friend of ours who never implemented the proper planning. Despite carrying millions of dollars of protection in various coverages, he was sued when one employee sexually harassed another employee. Though the business owner was not even present at the time of the harassment, the employer was forced to pay $2,000,000 in damages. This basically wiped out the business owner. Though he had the right to try and recover damages from the employee who was at fault, he knew the employee who earned $20,000 per year would never be able to pay even a fraction of the claim.

Even when a claim is insured, you must ask whether the insurance will fully cover the claim. A million-dollar liability policy does not mean much when you are sued for two million. With today's unpredictable, ludicrous jury awards, you cannot foresee what damages you may someday be forced to pay. Then, too, you may discover that liability insurance is not your complete answer to financial security.

There are countless policy exclusions; the inevitable loopholes that allow your insurance company to deny coverage. The many 'bad faith' claims now pending against insurance companies prove this point.

You cannot even be sure that your insurance company will be in business when you need them. Many asset protection specialists are now trying to protect the assets of scores of physicians in Ohio, New Jersey, and several other states whose insurance companies filed bankruptcy. These doctors thought that they were protected, but they are now exposed with little or no coverage. Many are in the middle of lawsuits! This could happen to you as well if you rely on someone else to take care of you.

No, we are not against liability insurance. In fact, we want our clients to have adequate insurance coverage because insurance is a good first line of defense in any asset protection program. Buy whatever liability insurance you can reasonably afford, but look upon insurance as a starting point. Liability insurance cannot take the place of a good asset protection plan, which you will need to protect yourself from any type or any size claim. Asset protection planning is the only way to achieve complete financial safety.

Myth #4: "Asset protection is too costly. I can't afford it."

Protecting your assets is not too costly, and probably will not take more than a few hours of your time. Our experience shows that the average family can gain strong protection for their assets for only a few thousand dollars. We have protected significantly larger fortunes (over $25 million) for under $25,000, and there are many protective steps that cost you absolutely nothing.

If you get sued, how much would you then pay to avoid the time and aggravation that will go along with the lawsuit? Days (if not weeks) out of work handling legal requests, dollars spent on attorneys and expert witnesses, and potentially millions of dollars in awards (if you lose) are the downside of not implementing asset protection planning.

The upside of this planning is that most asset protection planning also offers the families of our clients additional benefits. The tools that we utilize can help eliminate unnecessary probate costs (which can cost up to 8% of the total gross estate), eliminate accidental disinheritances of children from previous marriages, reduce income taxes, and possibly help reduce business expenses (like traditional insurance premiums). In most cases, the savings a business experiences in the first one or two years make up for the lifetime of creditor protection this planning affords.

Myth #5: "My Corporation Protects Me."

Please understand that just because you operate your business as a corporation does not mean that your assets are protected from lawsuits and that you can rest easily. Here is what your corporation can and cannot do for you:

1. Corporations will not protect your corporation's assets (equipment, vehicles, land, buildings, franchise agreements, leaseholds, etc.) from claims that arise in the ordinary course of business of the corporation. Therefore, negligence on the part of any franchisee in the operation of his or her business, including slip and falls and ill-prepared food, threaten the franchise's assets themselves — even if you are incorporated;

2. Corporations will not protect your franchise assets nor your *personal assets* from certain types of claims. These would include actions for sexual harassment, civil rights violations (e.g., sexual or racial discrimination), and wrongful termination. If an action is brought against you for any of the foregoing, your business assets and personal assets

are both exposed to seizure by the plaintiff or judgment creditor. It does not matter that the cause of action arose in the ordinary course of business.

Myth #6: "I Can Just Give It Away If I Get Into Trouble."

Another common misconception is that you can just give it away or transfer your assets if you are sued. If this were the case, you could hide assets all day long. You wouldn't need an asset protection specialist. Rather, you would only need a shovel and some mapmaking skills so you could find your buried treasure later.

There are laws against fraudulent transfers or fraudulent conveyances. In a nutshell, if you make a transfer after the incident occurred (whether you knew about it or not), the judge has the discretion to rule it a fraudulent conveyance and order the asset to be returned to the transferor. The details of the fraudulent transfer statutes are beyond the scope of this book. However, you can find more detailed descriptions by visiting www.mywealthprotection.com to order *Wealth Protection: Build and Preserve Your Financial Fortress* and reading the asset protection chapters.

If you have been sued or suspect that you may be sued, there are things you can do to protect yourself. If you have a problem and fear that you may be on the wrong end of a large judgment, then we recommend you implement some type of planning immediately. Typically, these last minute strategies are considerably more risky and costly than the highly effective strategies that can be implemented when there are no risks lurking. The best advice we can give here is that you start your planning early, $5,000 to $10,000 spent now may save you hundreds of thousands — if not millions — of dollars when a problem eventually arises.

If your fast-food restaurant operation looks anything like any of the structures we have described above, then you will benefit greatly from this book. From an asset protection standpoint, we can help you structure your business and personal assets and perhaps afford you some tax relief in so doing.

To find out how best to implement asset protection strategies for your particular situation, continue reading, contact the authors, or meet the WPA member in your area.

CHAPTER FOUR

Asset Protection is a Sliding Scale

Now that we have discussed some of the asset protection myths in the previous chapter, we have one more misconception to clarify for you. Many people believe that an asset is either "protected" or "unprotected." This "black or white" analysis oversimplifies the field of asset protection. In fact, asset protection strategies vary from case to case and each individual client will present different issues and objectives.

The first goal of an experienced asset protection professional will be to get a client to avoid "bad habits." For a medical patient, bad habits might mean smoking, drinking too much or eating unhealthy foods. For a client of ours, bad habits might include owning property in your own name, owning property or assets jointly with a spouse, or operating a franchise restaurant with assets of the franchise unnecessarily exposed to lawsuits or taxes.

In fact, much like a physician who judges the severity of a client's illness, asset protection specialists use a rating system to determine the protection or vulnerability of a client's particular asset. The scale runs from -5 (totally vulnerable) to +5 (superior protection).

Negative Numbers for "Non-Planning" or "Adverse Planning"

When most clients initially come to see us, their asset planning scores negatively. For personal assets, they typically own them jointly (-3) or in their individual name (-5). Both of these ownership forms provide little, if no, protection from outside lawsuits and they may have additional tax and estate planning negatives as well. As you learned in the previous chapter, these forms of ownership, as well as having the spouse own the asset outright, are not effective methods of protecting assets.

In terms of business assets, the worst way to operate a business or to hold any assets would be in a general partnership (-5). Although

17

using a corporation or other legal entity may provide some protection, it never protects you from certain types of lawsuits such as sexual harassment. Thus, having business assets owned by that same legal entity is extremely unwise (-3).

Before we implement any sophisticated asset protection planning, we want to move the client from a -5 score to at least a neutral number. This means eliminating any of the "bad habits" named above. If you see yourself as a businessman who has business assets exposed and owns personal assets in your name or jointly with a spouse, you should talk to an asset protection advisor immediately. You don't want linger too long in the −3 or worse category because you have a higher than average risk of getting "sick."

What Kind Of Client Are You?

The most difficult question that arises in asset protection planning appears to be distinguishing those situations where asset protection is appropriate from those where it is not. Although this question may seem abstract in nature, the answer to this question appears to have compelling practical effects. The moral implications of creating an asset protection plan, including **who you are** and **what you have done**, may determine whether the plan ultimately succeeds or fails.

It must be understood that any judge or jury is likely to be influenced by moral considerations when determining whether or not to allow an asset protection structure to shield assets from a creditor. Much has been made recently of cases where the courts have ordered judgment debtors to assign assets over to their creditors in order to satisfy an outstanding judgment. Assignment can occur in a variety of ways, ranging from partition of limited partnership shares to a forced sale of corporate assets. In one case, the judgment debtors were ordered to send their offshore assets back to the United States to satisfy a judgment. When the debtors refused to do so, the court held them in contempt and sent them to jail until they complied with the order to return the assets. Interestingly, although the judgment debtors in this case were forced to serve several months in jail as a result of their contempt, they were ultimately released without having to return the millions of dollars to the United States to pay creditors. Some advisors view this case a failure since the clients spent six months in jail. Other advisors view this case as a success because the clients, despite being of extremely questionable character, never lost their millions. Whether you believe sitting in jail for a few months is worth millions or not is not really the point. The point is that the planning is awfully effective even where the clients are pretty bad people the courts really want to punish.

If there is one pattern or principle that can be gleaned from the line of decisions in this area, it may be this: the worse the conduct that results in the debt or judgment, the more likely it is that the courts will look for any technicality that may allow them to undo your asset protection plan. Hence, a person that has defrauded elderly people from their money is more likely to have an asset protection plan penetrated than is a person who has a large judgment entered against him/her because of an injury due to simple negligence. Applied to restaurant owners, this principle would render a restaurateur who has committed racial discrimination in employment practices far more vulnerable than one who, for instance, has a judgment entered for a "slip and fall." Without question, who you are and what you have done are factors to consider when consulting with an asset protection specialist. Now, let us discuss the differences between basic and more advanced asset protection planning.

Basic Asset Protection

Using the sick patient analogy, if a doctor sees a patient with a particular condition/disease, he will try to treat it. For us, we try to treat franchisees in a manner that will cure their lawsuit vulnerability. In this regard, we use particular structures to protect a franchisee's assets.

Keeping with the analogy, a doctor may not recommend surgery for a patient right away because the patient is not sick enough to warrant surgery. As this relates to asset protection, an asset protection advisor may not recommend the most protective structure for a client who doesn't need it. Perhaps, given that client's net worth and income, the cost of the most advanced structures may not be justified. In those instances, we may recommend the next best strategy — a slightly inferior, but cost-effective alternative.

If you are in such a situation, where you want good, basic, asset protection but do not want to pay for more advanced tools, then basic asset protection tools like family limited partnerships (FLPs) and limited liability companies (LLCs) should be used. Essentially, these tools will provide good asset protection against future lawsuits, allow you to maintain control, and can provide income and estate tax benefits in certain situations. For these reasons, we often call FLPs and LLCs the "building blocks" of a basic asset protection plan.

In essence, FLPs/LLCs will provide adequate asset protection and, when utilized correctly, afford you an asset protection score of +2. Another approach might be to protect the asset as well as the state statute allows and perhaps strengthen your bargaining position sufficiently to encourage the creditor to accept a settlement rather than pursue outright protection of the asset with more expensive tools. Obviously, the asset protection plan is reliant upon proper drafting of the requisite documents, proper maintenance and respect for formalities, and proper ownership arrangements. If all these are in place, the franchisee can enjoy basic asset protection for a relatively low cost.

Ultimate Asset Protection: Advanced Strategies

For many business owners, a basic asset protection plan, which has some potential vulnerability, is not good enough. A +2 on their asset protection score is not enough to give them the psychological comfort they want. Other clients may feel the extra expense of an advanced structure is worth it, especially when significant tax benefits may be achieved as well. For these reasons, these clients use advanced structures to put themselves at a +4 or +5, the ultimate asset protection scores. Like a doctor giving the ultimate medicine or most effective surgical procedure, asset protection consultants rely on a number of tools to provide ultimate asset protection. As you'll learn in upcoming chapters (or in articles or in our other books), these advanced tools include:

International Limited Liability Companies. If implemented in the right jurisdiction (e.g., the British West Indies), if properly structured, and if company assets are held offshore, foreign LLCs can be a +4. US-based creditors will have so many procedural hurdles and expenses to overcome before they can institute proceedings in certain foreign jurisdictions, they often settle for pennies on the dollar out of court.

Foreign Asset Protection Trusts ("FAPTs"). These are the elite tools of asset protection planning — the ultimate +5. When created in the right jurisdiction where US judgments are not respected, and where procedural hurdles are toughest, most US creditors will give up rather than even try to attack these structures.

Captive Insurance Companies. Structured domestically or internationally, these tools can also reach the +5 status, especially when owned by a second, separate entity such as an offshore LLC. Such companies can provide superior asset protection for a fast-food franchise and are extremely beneficial for tax planning as well.

Enhanced Debt Shields. These strategies are ideal for protecting equity in real estate, especially your personal residence. When structured properly, after-tax wealth can be built while protecting the real estate equity in a superior way (a +4 level of protection).

Funding of Exempt Assets. Each state law has assets that are absolutely exempt from creditor claims. Federal law also exempts certain assets. Because they are protected by statute, they enjoy a +4 to +5 level of protection. A good example of how state laws can protect assets can be found in Texas or Florida where the homestead exemptions are unlimited for personal residences, and the cash values in life insurance policies and annuities are completely protected. At the federal level, the law affords unlimited protection for ERISA-Qualified retirement plans such as defined benefit or profit-sharing plans.

Conclusion

Asset protection planning, like any sophisticated multi-disciplinary effort, is a matter of degree. Nothing in life is 100% certain and there are no guarantees under any area of the law. For asset protection planning, this adage holds true. In your asset protection plan, make sure you understand the cost and benefits of the various tools you employ as well as the type of asset protection client you are. It will not only help you protect the wealth you have already built, but may assist you in building greater after tax wealth for your retirement and beyond.

CHAPTER FIVE

Transferring & Transforming Assets

So far, we have discussed the need for asset protection, the common mistakes most franchise owners make, and the sliding scale of asset protection. A basic philosophy of asset protection is that you want to reduce your exposure to risk as cost-effectively and efficiently as possible. To reach this end, we want to take advantage of as many exempt assets (those protected under state or federal law) as possible since this asset protection is essentially "free" of any legal cost or annual maintenance costs.

The title of this chapter implies that the basic strategy of asset protection planning is to identify high risk assets and convert them into exempt assets or, at the very least, transfer these assets into entities that offer some protection. The simple analogy is one that we like to call "Left pocket, right pocket." Think of a favorite old pair of pants you own. The left pocket may have a hole in it while the right pocket has no hole. Why would you carry money or keys in your left pocket? Logically, you would put the valuable item(s) into your right pocket to keep them safe. Asset protection philosophy is no different than this simple "two pocket" example. You should make every attempt to carry as much of your valuable wealth in the pockets that do not have holes. This general tactic can be put to use in hundreds of different ways, limited only by the creativity of the asset protection advisor and the client.

This chapter examines the first such "tool" of asset protection: state and federal laws which already exist but which the vast majority of Americans do not use advantageously. As advisors, this is of particular concern to us because these "exemptions" are the most effective, least complicated, and least expensive asset protection alternatives.

Whether it is a homestead law, wage or pension exemption, life insurance exemption or other protective law, the government helps to protect particular assets. These particular protections are discussed in great detail in the Appendix. Keep in mind that the government's aid is at best inconsistent. These laws can be extremely valuable or virtually meaningless, depending on the creditor we are protecting against and the state in which you live. As with all asset protection strategies, maximizing protection under these laws can be tricky business that is best left to an experienced expert.

For clients who sought the advice of a Wealth Protection Specialist familiar with the laws and applicable cases of their states, there are many examples of simple and effective asset protection. Here are a few of the many ways individuals have successfully used this general tactic of transforming unprotected assets to +5 protected assets:

- A business owner obtained a second mortgage on the family's vacation home to reduce the mortgage on the primary home — thus protecting all of the equity under her state's homestead laws.

- Foreseeing creditor problems, a woman converted her vulnerable mutual funds into annuities and cash value life insurance (both of which are protected under her state's statutes).

- A California business owner converted his largely unprotected self-directed Individual Retirement Account ("IRA") into an ERISA-qualified Profit Sharing Plan protected by federal law.

- A franchise owner had to sell his homestead-protected home for financial reasons, just as another creditor threatened to sue. He transferred the sale proceeds directly into exempt assets — in his case, annuities. Thus, we have a corollary tactic: when selling exempt assets, direct funds into another exempt asset.

Conclusion

Asset protection is most effective when a variety of strategies are implemented. You don't want to "put all your eggs in one basket." Some of the most effective strategies involve the use of exempt assets.

In depth discussions of a number of exemptions are given in the Appendix and an even more comprehensive discussion is offered in *Wealth Protection: Build and Preserve Your Financial Fortress* (available at **www.mywealthprotection.com**). It is strongly suggested that you review the exemptions in the Appendix as a precursor to the most important part of your planning. It is also important to remember that an important component of the asset protection process is to work with a team of Wealth Protection Specialists who are familiar with your state's exemptions and who have experience integrating asset protection planning into estate planning, retirement planning, and financial planning so your family can get the most out of your plan. Realistically, you will not be able to complete 100% of your asset protection planning with exempt assets because businesses don't have these exemptions available to them. As a result, we will explore valuable legal strategies in the next few chapters.

CHAPTER SIX

Asset Protection Building Blocks

In the right states for clients who are open to reallocating their investments, personal asset protection can be achieved almost entirely with state and federally-exempt assets. For business owners, there is no way to protect against creditors without the basic building blocks of any asset protection plan — the limited liability company (LLC) and family limited partnership (FLP). In this chapter, we will discuss how these tools are used to shield the typical franchise owner's assets.

LLCs and FLPs: Twin Asset Protection Powerhouses

Of all the legal tools we use to shield assets, by far the two most used are limited liability companies (LLCs) and family limited partnerships (FLPs). Of course, having family members play a role is typical — that's why we use the word "family" in front of the LP. However, using family members in this way is NOT required. Whether or not you involve family members, these tools can provide extraordinary asset protection. For purposes of this writing, we will use the abbreviations LLCs and FLPs throughout.

We have combined these two tools in our discussion because they are so similar. You can think of them as closely related, like brothers or sisters, as they share many of their best characteristics. In fact, unless we make the point otherwise, we will use these terms interchangeably — if we refer to a FLP, you can assume that an LLC could have been used and *vice versa.*

Similarities Between the FLP and the LLC

1. They both are legal entities certified under state law

Both tools are legal entities governed by the state law in the state where the entity is formed. Many of these laws are identical, as they are modeled after the Uniform LP and LLC Acts, which have been adopted at least partially by every state.

2. They have two levels of ownership

Both entities allow for two levels of ownership. At one level is "active ownership," where active owners have 100% control of the entity and its assets. In the FLP, the active owners are called "general partners" and with the LLC the active owners are called "managing members." As you may have already guessed, the second ownership level is passive ownership. The passive owners have little control of the entity and only limited rights. The passive owners are called "limited partners" in the FLP and "members" in the LLC. This bi-level structure allows a host of planning possibilities because clients can then use LLCs and FLPs to share ownership with family members without having to give away any practical control of the assets inside the structures.

3. They both have beneficial tax treatment

In terms of income taxes, both tools can elect for "pass through" taxation — meaning neither the FLP nor the LLC is liable for income taxes. Rather, the tax liability for any and all income or capital gains on LLC/FLP assets "passes through" to the owners (partners or members).

4. They have the beneficial 'charging order' asset protection benefit

While state laws do vary, those based on the Uniform Acts provide "charging order" protection to FLP and LLC owners. (See the discussion below to learn more). It is very important to choose a favorable jurisdiction for your FLP or LLC.

Two Big Differences Between the FLP and LLC

It is true that these two legal entities are practically identical and, in some situations, they are completely interchangeable. However, you should be very aware of the two significant differences. They are as follows:

1. Only the LLC can be used for a single owner

Most states now allow single-member (owner) LLCs, while a limited partnership in every state must have at least two owners. Thus, for single clients LLCs are often their only option.

2. The FLP's general partner has liability for the FLP

While a general partner has personal liability for the acts and debts of the FLP, a managing member has no such liability for his/her LLC. For this reason alone, asset protection experts always recommend using an LLC rather than an FLP when the entity will own "dangerous" assets or operate an active business.

Dangerous assets are those which a relatively high likelihood of creating liability. Common dangerous assets include active businesses, real estate (especially rental real estate), cars, RVs, trucks, boats, airplanes, interests in closely-held businesses, and others.

Safe assets, conversely, are those that are unlikely to lead to lawsuits. These include: cash, stocks, bonds, mutual funds, CDs, life insurance policies, checking or savings accounts, antiques, artwork, jewelry, licenses, copyrights, trademarks, and patents.

CAUTION: Each state handles franchise taxes differently. For this reason, you must not only speak to an attorney well-versed in corporate formations, but you must also meet with a Wealth Protection Specialist who is familiar with the eccentricities of the tax laws in your state. For example, at the time of this writing, the state of Texas imposes a franchise tax on LLCs that is equivalent to a percentage of gross revenue and a percentage of the asset value of an LLC but does not charge this tax to FLPs.

How LLCs/FLPs Protect Assets

LLCs and FLPs are outstanding asset protectors because the law gives a very specific and limited remedy to creditors coming after assets in either entity. When a personal creditor pursues you, and your assets are owned by an LLC/FLP, the creditor cannot seize the assets in the LLC/FLP. Under the Uniform Act provisions, a creditor of a limited partner (or LLC member) cannot reach into the LLC/FLP and take specific partnership assets — he can only get a "charging order" against your share of the LLC/FLP.

The Weaknesses of the Charging Order as a Remedy for Creditors

The charging order is a court order which instructs the LLC/FLP to pay the debtor's share of distributions to the creditor until the creditor's judgment is paid in full. While this may seem like a powerful remedy, consider its limitations:

1. Only Available After a Successful Lawsuit

First, the charging order is only available after the creditor has successfully sued you and won a judgment. Only then can your creditor ask the court for the charging order. While there is a threat even while a lawsuit is proceeding, the LLC/FLP assets are completely untouchable and available for you to use during the course of the lawsuit (as long as you avoid fraudulent transfers). If you protect against "future unforeseen claims" in advance, you will be very well protected.

2. Does Not Give Voting Rights — So You Stay in Complete Control

Despite the charging order, you remain the general partner of your FLP (or managing member of the LLC). You make all decisions about LLC/FLP assets; whether or not to sell, to distribute earnings to the partners or members, to shift ownership interests, etc. Your judgment creditor cannot vote you out because he cannot vote your shares. Thus, even after the creditor has a judgment against you, you still make all decisions concerning the operations of the LLC/FLP, including the decision to refuse to pay distributions to the owners. Why would you decide to pay distributions when you know that the creditor will get them?

3. The Creditor Pays the Tax Bill

The real "kicker" is how the charging order backfires on creditors for income tax purposes. Because taxes on LLC/FLP income are passed-through to the parties who are entitled to the income (assuming you choose partnership taxation and not corporate double taxation), the LLC/FLP does not pay tax. Each partner/member is responsible for his/her share of the LLC/FLP income. This income is taxable whether or not the income is actually paid. Because a creditor who gets a charging order against you "steps into your shoes" for income tax purposes with respect to the LLC/FLP, your creditor will get your tax bill and owe income taxes on your share of the LLC/FLP income. This tax liability exists even though the creditor never received the income. Remember, you and your spouse decide if and when to make distributions and you certainly won't make any distributions when there is a creditor with a charging order. With this extraordinary "poison pill," you may ask the creditor to sue your wife and kids too! If a creditor thinks he will get more money out of a cheap settlement than from elusive LLC/FLP distributions, he will be more inclined to settle.

Ancillary Benefits of LLC/FLPs

Philosophically, the top advisors we know (members of the Wealth Protection Alliance) always try to implement Wealth Protection Planning strategies that offer numerous benefits. We can generally offer, in addition to creditor protection, some desirable tax and estate planning benefits. The benefits you will receive will be based on your particular situation and goals. The following benefits may or may not pertain to your situation. If these benefits are of interest to you, consult a Wealth Protection Specialist to see what benefits you might achieve from planning with LLCs and FLPs.

Tax Benefits of Using LLCs/FLPs

LLCs and FLPs can be used to "bracket share" family members' lower tax rates, thereby reducing total income taxes paid by your family. As a result of the tax savings, the entire asset protection plan can pay for itself in just a year or two. Let's see how this works in another real life case study:

Case Study: Ronald and Wendy's LLC Reduces Taxes

Ronald and Wendy own several burger franchises and they own the land where the franchises operate. The land is worth approximately $1,000,000. They don't pay themselves rent for the property because they own both the land and the franchise. Fair market value of the lease, if they were to pay the rent, would be $100,000 per year. In a combined 40% state and federal tax bracket, their total income tax on this income would be $40,000. To reduce their taxes and protect their investment from potential lawsuits, they worked with a local Wealth Protection Specialist to set up an LLC.

Ronald and Wendy funded the LLC with their real estate (not including their home) and named themselves as managing members in order to maintain 100% control. Ronald and Wendy then signed a lease agreement between the franchise and their new Real Estate LLC. They gifted 90% of the membership interests (all non-managing) of the Real Estate LLC to their children. Under the LLC agreement, the children were taxed on their prorated share of the LLC's income — $90,000 per year. A portion of the LLC's taxable income will now be taxed at the children's lower tax rate. When the LLC assets now earn $100,000 in income, 90% of that income is now taxed at the children's rate of 15% while 10% of the LLC income will be taxed at the parents' rate of 40%. The family's tax savings will be as follows

$10,000 taxed at 40%	**$4,000**
$90,000 taxed at 15%	**$13,500**
Total Taxes Paid	**$17,500**
Total tax without the LLC:	**$40,000**
Total family income tax savings Per year with the LLC:	**$22,500**

In addition to the significant annual income tax savings, there are estate tax benefits and the real estate is now protected from any lawsuits against the franchise that arise from its operations or the acts of the owners or its employees. To explore how the strategy of using LLCs or FLPs can benefit you, please work with a Wealth Protection Specialist.

CHAPTER SEVEN

Proper Structuring Solves Problems in Advance

You have heard "an ounce of prevention is worth a pound of cure." This adage has never been more true than it is in the fields of asset protection, tax, retirement, and estate planning. It is crucial that you realize the necessity of shielding all of your assets (business and personal) BEFORE any liabilities against you, any co-owners, or your employees arise.

In fact, building a franchising empire without making a significant effort to "asset-protect" yourself is a fool's gamble because you risk not only your fast-food restaurant operation but all of your family's wealth on just one bad lawsuit against you or any of your employees. Do not "skimp" on your planning here — it is far too important! In this chapter, we will deal with business assets, leaving personal asset protection for a later chapter. In case the reasons for protecting your franchise are not clear yet, let us explain the three main reasons for asset protection:

---

3 Reasons Why You Must Shield Business Assets

1. Business assets are vulnerable to all types of claims
2. Business assets are vulnerable to claims against any individual owner or employee of the business
3. You can actually earn more money by protecting business assets

---

Business Assets Are Vulnerable to All Types of Claims

In addition to customers alleging slip & fall incidents and premises liability, you can be sued by your own employees, under theories such as sexual harassment, wrongful termination, age or gender discrimination, among many others. You can even be sued for acts of violence by one customer inflicted on another customer. These claims can be just as expensive and dangerous as the most serious negligence lawsuits. In some states, the *average* sexual harassment award is over $1 million.

Unfortunately, *without any advance planning, all of your business assets are exposed to any and all of the types of lawsuits named above.* Do you really want to expose all of your valuable business assets, such as your future receipts, valuable equipment, even your building or other real estate to all of these potential liabilities? Do you want to take the risk of having even one negligence lawsuit (or other type of claim) wiping out all of your assets? Not after you consider the following:

1. Business assets are vulnerable to claims against any of the franchise owners

If your franchise has the common legal structure of a corporation or general partnership, then your business assets are not only exposed to all of the types of claims named above, but they are also threatened by such claims against any of the owners working in the franchise. We say this because, in virtually every claim against a franchise owner for behavior in his/her position in the business, the franchise will also be named as a defendant in addition to the individual owner. This is true whether the claim is for wrongful termination, sexual harassment, or even from a car accident involving an auto leased through the business.

The question becomes: *if there are ways to avoid it, why would you expose you valuable business assets to all types of lawsuits against any of your partners or employees?* While this may seem like a silly question, less than one in every twenty of the business owners who have called us over the years had previously done planning to avoid these unnecessary risks.

2. Shielding assets can make you MORE money

As advisors who see the ramifications of not protecting assets, we typically recommend such planning for a client when it will cost them something — in terms of legal fees and costs. We believe that the benefit of protecting our clients' long term financial security is worth the relatively small cost upfront — as it often is with insurance.

What if such planning did not cost you anything but rather, made you more money? If this were the case, what would be holding you back from protecting yourself?

As you read the specific tactics of how to shield business assets, you will see two ways such planning can increase your cash flows: by increasing your real retirement income and reducing your income taxes during the years you are in operation. Both benefits result in a real cash flow increase for you, the franchise operator. *In this way, you are getting paid to shield your business assets. In some cases, this "payment" can be tens if not hundreds of thousands of dollars!* Again, why would you not do this?

Before we explain how to shield each of your business's key assets, and make money doing so, it is important that we review how most franchises in this country are structured (possibly even yours). Not surprisingly, in terms of asset protection and tax planning, this "typical structure" is *the worst possible way to operate your business.*

Unfortunately, most accountants and attorneys don't specialize in asset protection or tax planning. As a result, they often suggest that clients implement the simplest planning structure. A plan requiring multiple legal entities (LLCs and FLPs) requires a bookkeeper, multiple tax returns, a lot of explanation, maintenance, and, in some cases, significant annual fees. It is much easier to just suggest you run everything from one company to keep the books simple. Let's look at how that structure might look:

Faulty Structuring of a Franchise

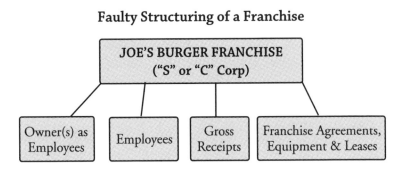

This diagram describes how nearly all franchises in the United States are organized. This is true of car dealers, fast food franchises, launderettes and basically every other franchise. More than likely, your franchise is organized in a very similar way. In this arrangement, there is one legal entity, typically a corporation (occasionally a sole proprietorship or general partnership), that operates the franchise and owns all of the key assets of the business. This would include future receipts, real estate, and any valuable equipment. Of course, as you have learned by now, this is the worst possible way to run a franchise in terms of asset protection. All of the franchise assets are exposed to any type of claim against any of the owners or employees.

The goal is to help you restructure your franchise from the diagram above to the one at the end of this chapter that illustrates an ideal franchise structure. From this point until then, we will show you how to implement a very simple tactic in four different ways. The tactic:

DO NOT HAVE YOUR OPERATING ENTITY OWN ANY VALUABLE BUSINESS ASSETS.

The statement above may be very simple, but its application is a bit more complex. Let's take a look at how this works:

Tactic One: Shield Your Income Stream

As noted above, your franchise's revenue stream is likely to be the most vulnerable of all your business assets — and its protection should be your first asset protection concern. This asset is so vulnerable because (1) the receipts are in the name of the franchise, so any claim against an owner or the franchise itself is a threat; and (2) a creditor can easily place a lien on the receipts, thereby gaining the right to payment as the receipts are collected.

For these reasons, shielding your revenue stream is an important priority. How can this protection be achieved? It is accomplished either by revenue factoring or financing — tactics that shield revenues from lawsuits and put more dollars in your retirement funds along the way. Let's see how this works.

Basic Overview — Financing Future Estimated Receipts

Financing means that you will "borrow" against your future receipts (thus removing the asset from the franchise) and distribute the proceeds to you or any other owner to hold in your own asset-protected accounts. Of course, this will result in a tax liability to each owner for receiving the payment from the business. Also, this transaction can be done ONCE for a stable business and a liability will constantly sit on the books against the cash assets of the franchise. All you have to do is pay the interest on the loan. Of course, in an ideal setting, you are using the loan proceeds to generate income that is greater than the after tax cost of the financing arrangement.

Typical Financing Arrangement

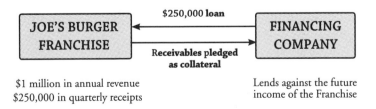

$250,000 **loan**

JOE'S BURGER FRANCHISE ← → **FINANCING COMPANY**

Receivables pledged as collateral

$1 million in annual revenue
$250,000 in quarterly receipts

Lends against the future income of the Franchise

There is another solution to this problem that is beyond the scope of discussion in this book. It must be noted that this book is not meant to be a treatise in advanced asset protection or tax-planning strategies — especially when complex tax issues are involved. If you are interested in learning more about effective financing strategies, feel free to contact the authors. Let it suffice that if done correctly, a well-conceived debt shield can protect future receipts from creditors, reduce current tax liabilities, and increase after-tax retirement income to each owner by roughly 20% (which could be more for those under 50 years of age).

Tactic Two: Separate Valuable Real Estate & Reduce Taxes

In working with successful business owners nationwide, we have found that it is common for the business to own the building in which it operates. This is even true for restaurant owners. Once again, too often this asset is owned by the owners through the same legal entity that is operating the franchise.

There are three reasons to separate the ownership of the real estate (RE) from the operating franchise. First, like the franchise revenues, the RE is a valuable asset that should be isolated from any liability created by the franchise or its owners. The reason why has been explained already with regard to revenues. Second, the RE itself may cause liability — most likely, slip and fall claims from those coming and going on the premises. If the RE and the restaurant are operated by the same legal entity — both "eggs" are in the same "basket," exposing each to the other's potential liabilities.

By separating the RE from the franchise, you have also asset-protected the franchise better — by isolating it from any premises liability created by the RE. This way, each entity is a superior shield and the valuable "eggs" of the franchise, the RE and the Franchise Agreements, are not in the same "basket". As an added measure of asset protection, one could also utilize the Debt Shield strategy (discussed later) for your restaurant RE.

What Does This Involve?

The actual tactic of separating ownership simply involves creating a new limited liability company (LLC) and transferring ownership of the real estate to the LLC. The restaurant will then lease the real estate from the LLC and actually pay market-value rent to the LLC. Because the RE is no longer owned by the operating franchise, customers or employees suing the franchise have no claim against this LLC owning the real estate. Moreover, and as you will learn in the next section, any claims against you or your partners cannot penetrate this LLC either, so the RE is immune to lawsuits against you as well. So long as the transfer to the LLC is done properly, and the formalities of the new arrangement are respected (i.e., the restaurant pays rent to the LLC), this protection will hold.

Note: As long as the ownership of the franchise/C-Corp and the Real Estate LLC are the same, assets can be transferred rather easily and most likely without additional taxation. If the ownership of both entities is not exactly the same, further planning related to real property valuation and taxation may be required. To be safe, check with a qualified Wealth Protection Specialist in your area first.

Your Financial Incentive

As with the isolation of your revenue stream, asset protection should be the primary goal of shielding the real estate. Similar to what we implemented when we protected the revenues, there can also be significant financial benefit to be enjoyed when it is combined with other tax-reduction tactics that protect business assets too. Rather than spend too much time on these here, we will briefly outline them. Of course, if you would like more information on how these tactics might work for you, please contact us directly in Los Angeles at 310-536-0700 or at 800-554-7233 if you are anywhere else.

In short, the best way to reduce income taxes while protecting your real estate is explained on the following page. For simplicity sake, we will assume that you are a one owner franchise (although these techniques work equally as well for multiple-owner franchises):

Own your business RE through an LLC that is initially owned by you and your spouse. Over time, you can gift ownership interests to children, while maintaining 100% control of the LLC and the RE (please refer to the discussion on shielding personal assets for more on how LLCs work). Once the children are over the age of 14, their percentage of the LLC income will be taxed at their low rates. If you can take full advantage of this, tens of thousands of dollars in income taxes can be saved each year. Stretched out over a career, the savings (and growth on saved dollars) can reach well into the six figures. For more on how this "bracket sharing" works, please refer to the discussion regarding tax benefits in Chapter 6.

Tactic Three: Separate Valuable Equipment & Reduce Taxes

Much more common than a franchise owning real estate is one that owns valuable equipment such as expensive stoves and franchise agreements. In today's world, the equipment of a restaurant franchise can be quite valuable in and of itself. To subject these assets to the potential liabilities of the restaurant makes no more sense than to do so for the real estate. This tactic, therefore, is extremely important.

This tactic is virtually identical to the real estate tactic above. It is implemented the same way by creating an additional LLC, the "equipment LLC," which takes ownership of these assets and then leases them back to the operating restaurant.

Moreover, as with the RE, tax benefits can be gained by combining these LLC's with "bracket sharing" or with the use of a CIC. (**Note:** It must be understood that before undertaking this strategy, one must consider the amount of tax deductions for depreciation on heavy equipment that are being claimed and make certain that the leasing expenses paid to the "equipment LLC" are sufficient to ensure that the "equipment LLC" is able to take full advantage of such deductions).

Tactic Four — Separate Franchise Agreements

Typically, the franchise owner will directly contract with the national office for assumption of the franchise rights. If the franchise owner has purchased the franchise business from a prior owner, then the client will typically have signed an "Assumption" or "Assignment" of the franchise agreement from the franchise's prior owner. Either way, the client will usually assume the obligations of the franchise agreement either individually or through his "S" or "C" corporation and therein lies the danger.

Assuming the foregoing scenario, what would happen to these franchise agreements in the event that a major liability were to arise in the operation of the restaurant? The answer is that these agreements, like every other asset that is in the name of the franchise owner or the corporation, would be subject to seizure, attachment, or receivership at the hands of a creditor or plaintiff. A creditor could literally assume complete control of the restaurant's operation or, if necessary, sell the rights under the franchise agreement to a qualified prospective buyer.

It is therefore recommended that the franchise owner also shift ownership, or all rights to operate under the franchise agreement, to a separate LLC or limited partnership and then lease or assign the right to operate under the franchise agreement to the corporation or individual client operating the restaurant. In this way, if the restaurant has a pending or actual liability the franchise owner can still operate a restaurant simply by setting up a new corporation or LLC to operate the restaurant. Moreover, the franchise owner would still have the right to sell his or her franchise rights to a prospective buyer and keep the proceeds from this sale — a far preferable outcome to having your creditor sell the franchise rights to buyer and apply the proceeds toward satisfaction of a judgment.

Putting It All Together: The Franchise as Financial Fortress

If you were to implement all four of the tactics discussed, your franchise restaurant would now look like this:

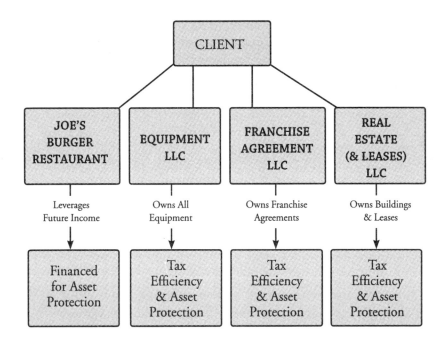

Now, any claims against any of the owners or the franchise itself — for slip and fall accidents or other claims — would not threaten the franchise's revenue stream, its real estate, its valuable equipment or its franchise rights. In this way, the real worth of the franchise would be completely shielded! In addition, you would be leveraging your future revenue receipts by putting away significantly more funds for retirement (either through factoring or financing) and you could reduce your income taxes by paying rent on your franchise RE and equipment through the use of LLCs. *Hence, you are now better-protected, wealthier, and ideally positioned to handle estate planning and business succession needs.* Why wouldn't you do this? The only possible obstacle would be the ongoing costs of such an arrangement.

Typically, the cost of implementing such a strategy depends on several factors, including but not limited to:

- what an attorney would charge to set up the proposed structure;

- what additional accounting fees would be incurred to do the tax filings for each of the new entities; and

- the ongoing franchise fees or taxes that are assessed in the jurisdiction where the entities are established.

In the event that the ongoing costs become overly burdensome, one could start by simply establishing one LLC and placing all of the franchise assets (real estate, leases, equipment, etc.) into one LLC until such time as it is feasible to separate each valuable asset into its own LLC. In any event, it is *critical that the restaurant franchisee understand that the ultimate goal of any business asset planning is, at the very least, to "strip" the restaurant operation of its assets so that the only asset remaining in its ownership or control is — at most — its revenue stream.*

CHAPTER EIGHT

Protection from Your Partners & Their Families

Do you recall the saying about the devil you know and the devil you don't know? The gist of the saying is that the devil you know is far less dangerous because you can "see him coming." Most franchise owners fail to address most creditor risks. A few of the savvy owners address the devil they do know — employee and customer lawsuits. Nobody protects against the devils they don't know. In this chapter, we will discuss the devil you didn't realize was even there — your partner's family.

If you are lucky enough to have found a business partner you trust, then you are steps ahead of most people in your shoes. If you found a great business partner, then you are very lucky to have basically won a lottery. What you didn't do when you picked your business partner was interview your partner's spouse and children. Would you like to have them as your next partner? If the answer is "No," then you have to plan for all possible alternatives. The biggest mistake business owners make when it comes to business succession is not having an adequate "Buy-Sell" agreement.

Why the Buy/Sell Agreement Is So Crucial

As owner of a private business, professional practice, or other venture, you likely spend 10 hours per day and six or seven days per week to get your business to the point where it can provide a measure of security for your family. We know because we have been there ourselves. Nonetheless, if you ignore one fundamental legal contract, all of your work may be in jeopardy. That contract, a key to your business Wealth Protection plan, is the Buy/Sell agreement. Succinctly put, the "Buy/Sell" agreement is a must for any partner or shareholder in a private company.

Please consider the following:

- What happens if one of my partners dies? Do I want my partner's heirs as partners? If not, how do I find the money to buy them out?

- What happens to my share of the business if I want out of the business or want to retire?

- What happens if any of my partners become disabled, or they get divorced? Will their spouse or ex-spouse become my partner?

- What happens to my family if I die or become disabled? How will I ensure that they get a fair amount for their share of the business?

Let's look at a quick case study involving only one of the many areas where a buy/sell agreement has great utility. As you'll see, it is a pretty typical case:

Case Study: When a 2-Person Firm Loses a Partner

Fred and Bob are equal owners of two pizza parlor franchises that generate $3,000,000 in annual revenues. Over the years, Fred's expertise has been in the area of restaurant operations while Bob has been responsible for the partnership's finances and marketing. Their overall profitability is due to their joint efforts. If Fred were to die prematurely, Bob might have to hire a new employee to fill Fred's position — or promote someone and fill the position. With the new hire, it's unlikely that the person could duplicate Fred's results.

At the same time, Fred's widow would want to continue to take the same money out of the business that Fred received. In fact, if Fred's widow is raising a young family or has children in college, she may have to force a sale of the business at distressed prices just to meet her needs. Perhaps Fred's son is also in the business and has his own ideas on how things should be done.

Fred's wife wants to see her son take his father's place. It doesn't matter that he is incompetent.

Now you see the many problems that can arise. Needless to say, it may be impossible for Bob to continue a profitable business under such circumstances. Only by planning ahead can you and your partners answer these questions in a way that all parties are satisfied and the business will be sustained. The best tool for solving these dilemmas is a well-conceived buy/sell agreement.

Buy/Sell Basics

There are various types of buy/sell agreements, which we will discuss below. Nonetheless, there are some basics regarding all buy/sell agreements which that can apply to any type of business — specifically the benefit different stakeholders can realize when one is in place. Buy/sell agreements can be used for corporations ("S" and "C"), partnerships, limited partnerships, limited liability companies ("LLC") and other entities as well. For these discussions, we will use the words "business owner" generically to mean any type of business owner (i.e., shareholder in a corporation, partner in a partnership, member in a LLC, etc).

A. Benefits to the Business and Remaining Owners

From the standpoint of the business and remaining partners, a properly planned buy/sell agreement will provide the orderly continuation of the ownership and control of the business upon the death, disability, divorce, or bankruptcy of any owner. The buy-sell can also remove any discrepancies in the value of the shares if one owner desires to sell his/her ownership share.

The buy/sell can prevent unwanted outsiders from becoming owners and can eliminate the need for negotiation with surviving spouses and/or children. The agreement may also perform the role of a succession plan, providing for continuity or orderly succession of business management. As discussed below, the buy/sell agreement is often used in conjunction with life and disability insurance policies to effectively provide liquidity for the business to purchase outstanding ownership interests.

This, in effect, guarantees that the remaining owners will continue to control the business and be able to participate in the future growth of the business, while also preventing a competitor from purchasing ownership interests from a retired, disabled, or deceased owner, or surviving family members. This guarantees continuity of management in the business, which makes the business more attractive to customers, creditors, and employees.

B. Benefits to Each Owner

From the standpoint of the living business owner, the agreement can provide the individual partner with an opportunity to negotiate and obtain the fairest or best price for his/her share of the business. In the case of retirement or disability, the agreement can be a source of additional funds for each owner.

C. Benefits to Family Members

For a deceased owner's family, the existence of the buy/sell can assure the family or estate a liquid asset rather than an interest — often a minority interest at that — in a private business, which is extremely difficult to sell. This can be extremely important as the family is now burdened with estate tax payments. Further, the agreement itself may provide an estate tax valuation of their business interest, saving them the headache and expense of fighting the IRS on valuation.

In the event that an owner becomes disabled, the buy/sell guarantees that the disabled owner's family does not have to become involved in the business in order to protect the family's interest. Moreover, it liberates the disabled owner and his family from the risk of future business losses and creates funds which may be used to pay medical bills and expenses of his own family, thus protecting the rest of the family's estate. This, in turn, creates peace of mind because the disabled owner can rest in comfort knowing that he has maintained his investment in the business organization and does not have to continue to worry about its future.

D. Funding the Agreement

Where the agreement contemplates a buy-sell transaction at the happening time of an owner's death or disability, insurance policies are generally recommended to fund the transaction. There are many reasons for this, including the following:

- Insurance policies pay a pre-determined amount, with proceeds available at exactly the time when they are needed as a funding source (no liquidity concerns);

- Proceeds will be available regardless of the financial state of the business at that point (so long as premiums have been paid);

- The business "leverages" the cost of premiums to create the proceeds; hence, it costs the business less to buy insurance than to save money in a special buy-out fund;

- The economic risks of early death or premature disability of any owner are shifted to the insurer; and

- Insurance proceeds are paid to the owner/owner's family income-tax free

If the payment contemplated under the agreement is not a lump sum cash payment at closing, or is a periodic payment other than through a disability insurance policy, it is important to consider some type of security arrangement for the departing owner. These might include personal guarantees from remaining owners, mortgages or security interests in real estate, a bank standby letter of credit, or even collaterally assigned life insurance. It is critical that the owners negotiate the valuation of the business and any security agreement before there is any idea of which partner will die, divorce, or become disabled first. This way, each owner will be unprejudiced in determining what a fair buy-out is.

E. The Need For A Coordinated Team

Creating a buy/sell arrangement that fits a particular business requires expertise and experience. Expertise in areas of corporate and business law, tax law, insurance products, and valuation are all absolute requirements. Just as important is the experience in dealing with different owners and being able to negotiate and draft an agreement which that meets the needs of all parties involved.

Business owners typically make one of two key mistakes in deciding who should oversee the creation of a buy/sell arrangement: The first is that they choose a lawyer friend to create the strategy and draft the document rather than an expert in the area. The second common error is that they do not have a coordinated team to implement the plan.

Ideally, a coordinated buy/sell team would involve an experienced attorney creating these arrangements, a life or disability insurance professional who has worked on these issues before (especially with first to die life insurance), and a business appraisal firm, whose expertise may be needed continually in the future for annual business valuations.

Conclusion

As with any legal or insurance planning, the early bird is richly rewarded. No place is this more true than in buy/sell planning. The reason here is not so much economic, but political. If this planning is done before an owner is close to disability, divorce, retirement, or death, then all owners are in the same position of strength from a bargaining standpoint. This makes the negotiation of a standard deal for all owners a much easier and smoother process. Planning early for a buy/sell will truly benefit you, your family, and your business. Consider it an essential part of your Wealth Protection Planning.

CHAPTER NINE

Advanced Planning for Your Franchise & Family

As professionals who have been creating insurance companies for clients since the mid-1990's, we are quite familiar with the insurance, tax, and financial benefits of a varied number of alternative insurance arrangements. Given the state of the insurance market presently, it makes sense that we have seen an increasing number of business owners examine these alternatives.

In discussing a few of these arrangements here, we will begin with the captive or closely-held insurance company ("CIC").

The Captive or Closely-Held Insurance Company (CIC)

A CIC can be either a captive company (one owned by the owners of one restaurant franchise) or a closely-held company (owned by a few franchises). Beyond this distinction, the CIC can be used for both types of entities.

The CIC is a legitimate insurance company, registered in a legitimate international insurance jurisdiction, such as the British Virgin Islands, St. Kitts, Bermuda, or the U.S. Virgin Islands. Most CICs are established in these jurisdictions because of their favorable insurance laws and regulatory environment. Though these companies are typically created "offshore," the basis of their tax benefits are in the Internal Revenue Code of the United States. These companies elect to be taxed as U.S. entities and the funds of the CICs are typically maintained and managed in the mainland U.S. under the exclusive control of a U.S. taxpayer — you!

CIC as a Restaurant Franchise Insurer

The CIC can write liability insurance on its restaurant-related operations and its owners. The owners of the franchise pay tax-deductible premiums from their franchise businesses to the CIC (which they own).

The CIC will file an annual tax return with the IRS claiming 100% of its premiums, expenses, investment gains, losses, and other reportable amounts. If structured properly, companies that receive less than $1.2 million of annual premium are afforded a tax incentive by the IRS — they pay **0% tax** on insurance profits.

CIC as Risk Management Tool

In addition to possibly replacing traditional liability coverage, the franchisee's CIC has the flexibility to offer tax-deductible insurance against risks that the franchisee is already self-insuring but is NOT receiving a tax-deduction for doing so. By insuring deductibles, excess coverage amounts, or by insuring risks that are generally ignored by traditional liability policies (such as wrongful termination, sexual harassment, or racial discrimination actions under Title VII), the franchisee can create a pre-tax war chest to protect against future creditor claims. If you consider that the awards in some of these highly volatile areas can be over $1 million per case, franchisees would be well-advised to use the CIC for this purpose alone.

In essence, the question for the franchisee becomes: if you are going to use insurance to protect against risk, why give away the potential tax benefits to the insurance company when you could own the company and receive the tax benefits yourself? Let's examine this more closely.

Compared With Self-Insuring: Better Tax and Asset Protection

When you consider the risks that are not covered by your existing insurance policies (employment lawsuits, for example) you are essentially "going bare" and "naked" to creditors and their attorneys. For these claims, you are, in effect, self-insuring (i.e., betting that you won't have a claim and agreeing to pay it out of your pocket if you do). You put away after-tax funds every year, invest those funds (on a taxable basis), and, if you are ever sued, you will use those funds to pay for defense costs and for any settlement or jury award.

By creating your own CIC, you can do the same thing — put away money for a rainy day. However, by going through the formalities of creating a valid insurance company, you can realize annual tax deductions of up to $1,200,000 per year to accomplish this goal. *Premiums paid to the CIC are fully tax deductible, while amounts saved to "self-insure" are not. The CIC allows you to get a full deduction each year for protecting against the same risks from which you are already "self-insuring."*

From an asset protection standpoint, there is another problem with self insuring. When you "self-insure," the funds stay in your name or in the name of the franchise. Thus, they are at risk to any lawsuit claimants, creditors, divorce proceeding, bankruptcy trustees, etc. Simply put, there is no asset protection tool shielding the "self-insured" funds.

Conversely, by using the CIC, you have transferred such funds to an independently operated, fully-licensed insurance company. Because the law considers assets titled to the CIC to be the property of the prospective class of claimants and not the individual owners of the CIC, assets placed into the CIC are highly insulated from a franchisee's creditors. Any lawsuit, claim, divorce, tax, or other action against you or your business is completely separate from the CIC. In our opinion, the assets in the CIC are ideally protected against any litigation risks.

Taxation of CICs
If structured under either of the two relevant tax code provisions, the CIC can enjoy preferred tax status. Specifically, under these tax rules, the CIC may not be liable for tax on its premium income. In this way, while the franchisee and/or franchise deducts the premiums for policies written by the CIC, the CIC may not pay tax on the earnings of these premium dollars once the premiums are received. This beneficial tax treatment creates a tremendous investment opportunity for the franchisee.

No Loss Of Control

The CIC structure allows for complete control by the franchise owner. There is no need for the owner to trust any other person or entity with their assets. Moreover, while the CIC is typically established outside the U.S., the funds may remain in the U.S.

Avoiding Land-Mines

To create the CIC structure properly, it is critical that you work with professionals who have expertise in this area — especially the attorneys, accountants, and insurance managers that are involved. While this may mean that the CIC is more expensive than some of the cheaper alternatives being touted on the internet or at fly-by-night seminars, this is one area where "doing it right" is the only way to enjoy the CIC's benefits and stay out of trouble with the IRS and your state insurance commission.

Can You Afford a CIC?

As might be expected, the professionals most experienced in these matters charge significant fees for both the creation and maintenance of CICs. While the fees are significant for both individuals and restaurant franchises, the CIC is a viable and highly effective option in many circumstances because of its risk management, tax benefits, and asset protection features. You can typically expect to pay between $60,000 and $75,000 to create a CIC and between $20,000 and $30,000 per year to maintain the CIC. Obviously, these fees are very significant. For this reason, the CIC is really only a viable solution for a business (or groups of businesses) with $500,000 or more of annual profit. Before you rule out the CIC on price alone, you should consider what types of benefits you might realize if you avoid lawsuit judgments and you self insure within your own CIC.

Case Study: Mr. Pancakes, Inc.

Mr. Pancakes is a successful owner of two coffee shop franchises in California who has not been sued in 10 years of operation. Nonetheless, his liability premiums have increased steadily in recent years. When the premiums increased to $125,000 per year for $1 million of coverage for the restaurants, Mr. Pancakes was fed up. He had consulted a few attorneys and accountants and had sufficiently protected his assets before speaking with us. After reading our book, he called us, looking for an alternative to provide him coverage in a tax-wise manner. Mr. Pancakes established a CIC individually. Let's take a look at the benefit he enjoyed from his CIC:

Mr. Pancakes and his CIC: Creates Significant Funds

	Going Without Coverage	CIC Insures Risks
Liability Coverage	Self-insuring	Insures Multiple Risks
Operation Income (net)	$1,000,000	$1,000,000
CIC premium paid	$0	$500,000[a]
Taxable income	$1,000,000	$500,000
Federal & state income taxes[b]	$450,000	$225,000
Adjusted after-tax wealth[c]	$550,000	$275,000
Living expenses	$250,000	$250,000
Net After Tax Savings	$300,000	$25,000
Amount in CIC reserves	$0	$500,000[d]
Total Available if No Claims	$300,000	**$450,000**

[a] Deductible premiums can be as high as $1.2 million per year

[b] Assumes combined federal and state income taxes of 45%

[c] Exclusive of transactions costs

[d] Distributions to the owners of CIC are taxed at dividend rates (15% federal as of 2005)

Here, in just one year, Mr. Pancakes has added $150,000 of wealth because he owns his insurance company. He is in the same place coverage-wise he would have been in if he had just "gone bare" but now he has enjoyed a tax benefit for doing so. Furthermore, as his other business and personal assets were shielded in an asset protection plan, he became an ideal "Shallow Pocket" and was therefore an unattractive lawsuit target. It must be noted that Mr. Pancakes is under no obligation to submit a claim on his CIC policy if he is sued. Given the fact that he is so well shielded, he might not and thus force the party suing him to settle cheaply.

If you consider that many people who are in Mr. Pancakes' situation typically use a CIC for 5 to 20 years, you can see how the benefits to the business owner and his/her family (the CIC could be owned by children or a trust for the children if the business owner is interested in very efficient estate planning) could be in the millions of dollars! This is certainly worth the tens of thousands of dollars in annual fees.

"Defense Only" Policies

If, for some reason, a CIC is not an option for replacing existing coverage, but you still want to significantly reduce your business liability premium as well as your attractiveness to lawsuit claimants, then a "defense only" policy might be a good alternative for you.

This type of policy only covers expenses associated with defending a third party claims, such as attorneys' fees and court costs. It does not cover any part of an award or settlement. In this way, franchisees using this type of policy are still essentially "bare" for their actual liability.

One benefit of this policy is that you will pay significantly lower premiums than with an actual liability policy, for obvious reasons. Additionally, there are no insurance proceeds or "pot of gold" for a plaintiff's attorney to shoot for, so you become a less attractive lawsuit target. However, as we explained in the last section, because you are bare for liability, you will need to make sure you are in compliance with your state's laws and your Franchisor's rules regarding minimum liability coverage. A policy such as this may not qualify as liability insurance for these purposes.

What a CIC Cannot Do for You

At this point, many of you are probably wondering whether you can make the CIC concept work for you in the area of "traditional" insurance programs, such as Workers Compensation. Before you get too excited, please understand that the CIC is not a viable alternative to self-insure for Workers Compensation and many other traditional insurance programs (e.g., contractor liability). The reason for this is that traditional insurance programs must typically adhere to many legal requirements governed by state law. Workers Compensation laws, for example, require that the insurance company providing coverage to your company or franchise be a carrier "admitted" to operate within the state's jurisdiction. Because the legal standards necessary to becoming an "admitted carrier" in any given state are often formidable and cost-prohibitive, it is highly unlikely that any franchisee will ever find it desirable to undertake the time and expense of having their CIC become an admitted carrier for purposes of lawfully providing Workers Compensation coverage.

CHAPTER TEN

Protecting Personal Assets Completes the Planning

At this point, we will assume that you have made up your mind to turn your franchise into a Financial Fortress, protecting all of your future revenues, real estate, and valuable equipment from lawsuits. Now that you understand the financial and tax benefits you will gain by protecting yourself, you would be foolish not to engage in such planning. So we will assume that you have.

Now, you are half-way there — half-way to completing the planning you will need to implement prior to reducing or eliminating your liability coverage. The next step is to protect your personal assets — such as your home, savings accounts, securities accounts, rental real estate, and even valuable personal assets such as artwork and jewelry.

This subject certainly is an important one. We have already written two books that deal with this type of planning quite extensively, *Wealth Protection, MD,* and *Wealth Protection: Build & Preserve Your Financial Fortress.* We will attempt to summarize the key points of personal asset protection planning here.

Protecting Your Home

Along with retirement accounts, your home is likely the most valuable asset you have. Even beyond its pure financial value, your home has large psychological value as well. In fact, we find that most of our clients who engage in asset protection planning often begin with the question: "How can I protect my home?" That is why we thought it important to dedicate an entire section to discussing this asset and how to protect it from outside threats. Before we do, however, consider this short case study:

Case Study: Victor the Victim of Bad Luck and Poor Planning
Victor dreams of becoming the "Fried Chicken King" in his area of the country. He recently started a new franchise as a general partnership with another restaurateur with whom he

had worked and trained some years ago. Victor and his wife have a home worth $500,000, with a $200,000 mortgage balance. Victor also has $100,000 in a SEP-IRA from his earlier practice as an attorney. He has $150,000 in brokerage accounts. Victor's partner, whom we shall call Unlucky Lou, had the misfortune of being accused of sexual harassment by an attractive female co-worker. Initially, the co-worker was upset but not vindictive. She had no intention of suing the franchise. After a few conversations with an attorney, however, her opinion changed and she sued Lou, along with the franchise.

After a long 18 months of depositions and discovery, the case actually went to trial. The judgment was $2,000,000. The plaintiff seized Lou's $400,000 brokerage account. Lou still had $1,000,000 in the profit sharing plan from his prior job. Aware of the federal protection of the plan assets, Lou then filed bankruptcy to rid himself of the creditor. He did lose what little equity he had in his home along with his brokerage account, but he was able to save his biggest assets, his profit sharing plan and his cash value life insurance policies.

The plaintiff wasn't happy with the partial satisfaction of the judgment. She then went after the franchise and its other owners (Victor) for the remainder. Under the premise of joint and several liability with the general partnership, Victor still had to personally come up with the remainder. Victor's attorney could not protect him. Victor couldn't believe this. He asked his attorney if he could declare bankruptcy to save his assets. Victor unfortunately found out the hard way that his SEP-IRA, home, and brokerage accounts were all to be largely lost in this lawsuit. In actuality, they were all lost but for a small amount of the IRA account.

Victor had met the employee only once, but through the miracles of litigation and creativity of the suing attorney, Victor lost everything. What could he have done? We have previously discussed the advanced strategies to protect IRAs, the revenues of the franchise, and the personally-owned brokerage accounts. The focus of this article is to discuss how both Lou and Victor could have protected their homes.

While the above case study is extreme, the need to protect the home is an important one. The precise game plan for you depends on the facts and circumstances of your situation. The most common tools we use to shield a client's home from potential creditors are set forth below. You have previously seen how state Homestead laws can afford varying degrees of protection for the home but there are other tools that can also serve to protect your home. They are as follows:

Tenancy by the Entirety

In states like Arizona (and others), you can file to have your home owned by Tenancy by the Entirety (T/E). Theoretically, this means that only a creditor who has a claim against both you and your spouse can take the home if it is titled this way. T/E is not automatic. You have to record a deed designating that your home is titled this way. Also, there has been a case when a litigant successfully penetrated a T/E and took a home from a couple because the couple had at least one joint creditor (it was a credit card with both of their names on it). Because of this case, we hesitate to consider T/E as a very strong protector — though we do admit it is much better than simple joint ownership. Again, the key here is to work with a local asset protection specialist to make sure that the T/E protection in your state is reliable. If the T/E law is absolutely solid in your state, then this ownership form can be a +3 to +4 on the scale.

Qualified Personal Residence Trusts (QPRTs)

When using a QPRT, you transfer ownership of the home to the QPRT irrevocably. While this is certainly effective for both asset protection and estate planning purposes, it comes with a significant cost — you no longer own your home and you also lose the $250,000 capital gain exclusion ($500,000 for married couples) if the Trust sells the home later. In fact, when the term of years is up (typically, 10 years), you have to pay rent to the trust just to live in the home. Also, homes with mortgages on them present further tax difficulties as well. For these reasons, while the QPRT is a strong asset protection tool, we typically do not advise using it for most clients whose main concern is asset protection, rather than estate planning. Nevertheless, in terms of pure asset protection benefits, a QPRT gets a +4 or +5 level of protection if it can be implemented correctly.

Debt Shields

The debt shield can be the most effective way to shield the equity of the home. Essentially, using a debt shield means getting a loan against most of the equity in your home. Once in place, the mortgage becomes a powerful asset protection device because few creditors or plaintiff's lawyers will target an asset where a bank is the "first-in-line" creditor. The large mortgage thus makes your home a very undesirable target.

For many clients, this is counter-intuitive — they want to pay down the mortgage as much as possible. While this may have emotional appeal for asset protection purposes, it is the exact opposite of what most of you want to do.

To help people protect their home equity, one financial institution has designed an ideal "debt shield" program for their clients. The bank loans the client the funds up to 90% of the value of the home and then files a mortgage (1st, 2nd or even 3rd) to "eat up" any available equity. Now the home is protected.

The loan funds are placed in an asset-protected trust — one drafted for the client by an asset protection attorney. Those funds are owned by the trust and, under the loan documents, required to be placed in the bank's CD account. Further, the bank contractually guarantees that its loan rate will be only 1% more than its CD rate — meaning that this structure will only cost you 1% of the home equity to implement (plus legal fees). When you retire or feel that the threat to the home has diminished, the CD account pays off the loan and the mortgage is released. This certainly has proven to be attractive to many looking to shield the home.

The Enhanced Debt Shield

In the basic debt shield above, there is a real cost to the loan versus the investment — a shortfall of 1% per year. What if the funds you gain by shielding your home could be invested in a way that you MAKE more than the loan interest? In this way, you would make money by shielding the home (or build equity faster). Certainly, this is possible, in many states.

In some states, certain investment classes are asset-protected under state law. What is the most common? Annuities and cash value life insurance policies are protected in states like New York, Florida, and Ohio, among others. In states such as these, you could take a loan for 5% or 6% (tax-deductible partially or totally) and be able to invest in an annuity or insurance policy that credits 5% to 7% (tax-deferred). When you consider that the mortgage interest may be tax deductible, the true after-tax "cost" to you may be as little as 2.5% to 4%. If your asset protected investment returns approximately 6% (many life insurance policies have guaranteed minimum crediting rates of 3% or 4%) and you are paying only 3% or 4% (after taxes) in interest, you can actually make money while protecting your castle.

Conclusion

For most families, there is no more important asset than the home. If you are concerned about protecting your home, you should speak to an asset protection specialist to make sure the barbarians at the gate of your family's castle can do nothing more than make a lot of noise and cannot disrupt your quality of life.

Protecting Your Personal Assets

We have previously explained the basic strategy for using FLPs and LLCs — transferring title of your assets to the FLP/LLC so they will be protected from your creditors. This is basic "outside protection" from creditors and lawsuits because assets inside the FLP/LLC are protected against outside threats posed by third party lawsuits and creditors. Beyond this, please consider the following:

Separate Safe from Dangerous Assets.

Dangerous assets are those with a relatively high risk of liability. Common dangerous assets include real estate, particularly rental real estate, automobiles, trucks, aircraft, boats, and interests in closely-held businesses. Safe assets, conversely, are those that are unlikely to cause lawsuits. Typical safe assets include investment portfolios, cash accounts, artwork, jewelry, licenses, franchise agreements, copyrights, trademarks, and patents. As we have indicated earlier, dangerous assets should be owned by an LLC rather than an FLP because LLCs protect all owners from liability, while an FLP exposes the general partner's interests in the partnership as well as the general partner's personal assets. Following this logic, it makes sense to isolate safe assets from dangerous ones by isolating them into separate LLCs. If we are constrained to using an FLP, it is probably best to have the position of Managing General partner assumed by a corporation or an LLC.

Don't Put All of Your Eggs in One Basket.

We never know when a court of law is going to make a surprise departure or deviate from accepted legal norms or precedents. If any asset within a single FLP/LLC causes a lawsuit, all assets owned by that entity could still be vulnerable to seizure. By using multiple LLCs or FLPs, you will better protect each of your assets or "eggs." This also makes it more difficult for any creditor to come after your entire wealth or cluster of assets. In effect, creditors must conduct more investigation, prepare more legal discovery and file more motions in court, and perhaps even travel to different states to discern your asset structure. The simple rule is thus: the more entities used to own assets, the more difficult it will be for your creditors to attack your wealth. The result is that creditors, under such circumstances, are far more likely to agree to settlements favorable to you and your family.

Putting it Together: An LLC/FLP Case Study

Now that you understand how LLCs and FLPs work, let's take a look at a real case showing how these tools can be used to shield your assets from lawsuits. Let's examine the case of Harry Gump, a 53-year-old who owns a chain of taco houses and his wife Wilma, a school teacher, who have two teen-aged children and have the following assets:

Gump Family Balance Sheet

	Asset	Equity
Safe Assets	Home	$550,000
	Cash	$50,000
	Mutual Funds	$550,000
	Non-Managing LLC Interests	$600,000
	Antiques	$20,000
	Total Safe Equity	$1,770,000
Dangerous Assets	Franchise Property	$275,000
	Rental Real Estate	$255,000
	Business Equipment	$50,000
	Total Dangerous Equity	$580,000
	TOTAL EQUITY	**$2,350,000**

To provide the Gump's with maximum financial security using FLPs/LLCs, we use between two and four entities. Let us examine each:

Tool #1: "Gump Safe Asset FLP"

Owns: Cash, mutual funds, business interest and antiques.

Total value = $1,220,000

Interests:	Mr. Gump 1% owner as managing member; 48% as member
	Mrs. Gump 1% owner as managing member; 48% as member
	Each child 1% as members

Strategy: By isolating safe assets from dangerous assets, we ensure their security. Also, the charging order protections shield the assets from any claims against Mr. Gump for tort claims or otherwise. Moreover, because Mr. and Mrs. Gump are general partners, they have 100% control of the FLP and all FLP assets. They are more comfortable with this ownership arrangement.

Result: All $1,220,000 is now safe from creditors or lawsuits. The Gumps may decide to gift more to the children for estate and possible income tax reduction.

Tool #2: "Gump Dangerous Asset LLC"

| Owns: | Franchise property, rental real estate, & equipment. Total value = $580,000 |

| Interests: | Mr. Gump 1% owner as managing member; 49% as member |
| | Mrs. Gump 1% owner as managing member; 49% as member |

Strategy: These assets are dangerous because of the likelihood of lawsuits from tenants, customers, or neighbors. While one LLC owned both pieces of real estate and the equipment, a strong argument can be made to set up separate LLCs for each property and even one for the equipment.

Result: Any lawsuit arising from the rental property is isolated to the condos. All other wealth is shielded. Further, the equity in the rental property is protected against claims against Mr. Gump from the operation of his fast-food restaurant.

Conclusion

FLPs and LLCs are the two most utilized and most flexible legal tools we use to protect assets. It would be astounding if you did not use at least one of these tools as part of your Wealth Protection plan.

CHAPTER ELEVEN

Your Next Step: Take Action

As we stated at the outset of this book, our goal was to make you aware of the risks you face and to offer you practical options to deal with the present liability and tax crisis. Specifically, we focused on:

1. Solutions to protect your business and personal assets from all creditor threats — an absolute necessity for any business owner if you are interested in keeping what is rightfully yours;

2. Business strategies that enhance your business's profitability and reduce unnecessary income, capital gains, and estate taxes;

3. Practical combinations of the financial and legal strategies that offer personal and business benefits when properly integrated into your existing comprehensive Wealth Protection Plan.

We believe we have done our job. Even still, nothing you read in this book does you any good if you don't take action. If you want to reduce your liability exposure to all types of claims, reduce your insurance premiums, reduce income taxes, and increase your retirement income, we have given you strategies for doing so. Now comes your part.

First you should assess your situation. Speak to your partners and your spouse about shielding business and personal assets. Second, contact a qualified Wealth Protection Specialist to help you analyze your situation and create a plan for the businesses and for your personal assets. Chapter 12 and 13 describe how to do this through the Wealth Protection Alliance office in your area.

Third, systematically review your plan. We typically ask all of our clients to carve out one afternoon per month to sit down with advisors to review different aspects of their plan. By doing so, they stay on top of changes in the law and changes in their own financial situations without ever falling too far behind.

These are the questions you should be asking and the actions you should be taking. In the final analysis, you, your business, and your family will gain if you act, so act *now*.

If you would like the authors to review your current situation, you can request a meeting by completing the data form in Appendix B and faxing it to our offices at (888) 317-9896. Someone from our offices will call you immediately to schedule a time to go over your situation.

If you wish to meet with someone local, we will gladly refer you to a member of the Wealth Protection Alliance in your area. This expert will be able to bring you a team of advisors to help you with most of your planning needs. To learn more about the WPA, please read chapters 12 and 13 and Appendix I.

CHAPTER TWELVE

What is the Wealth Protection Alliance?

The Wealth Protection Alliance is a national network of independent financial planners, attorneys and accountants who work collaboratively as a multidisciplinary team to bring comprehensive integrated asset protection, tax reduction, insurance and investment planning and business succession solutions to business owners and high net worth families.

The Wealth Protection Alliance (WPA) is a high-end boutique planning network. The WPA does not advertise or recruit advisors. The growth of our organization is a result of word-of-mouth referrals and through our in-depth educational programs. In the last few years, the WPA has expanded into 50 markets nationwide. Though the WPA may not have an office in your town, we do have professionals in our network who are licensed in all 50 states. We recognize that it may be more convenient to work with someone whose office is only 2 miles from your home, many of the WPA's clients are willing to sacrifice a little convenience for the level of attention, experience and expertise that the members of the WPA offer them in the planning and implementation process.

The WPA was created by Chris Jarvis and David Mandell of Jarvis and Mandell and Dale Edwards of Agilis Benefit Services. Their combined experiences and careers in the fields of actuarial science, law, investment banking, financial planning, investment advisory services and insurance helped them develop their vision of integrated wealth protection planning.

Franchise Owners (or those of you who would like to "franchise" your wealth and build more for you and your family) appreciate the value of having specialists in different areas to help them reach their financial goals. When you need a doctor, you don't go to the obstetrician for your open-heart surgery. So, we recommend that you seek advisors who are experienced at handling your particular creditor protection, tax minimization, retirement and business succession needs. If your situation involves a particular problem that requires specific expertise, the WPA member in your area has access to over 200 professionals nationwide. When you work with someone at the WPA, this "team of experts" approach is what we offer you.

What do you get through the Wealth Protection Alliance?

First, you get a local team of advisors:

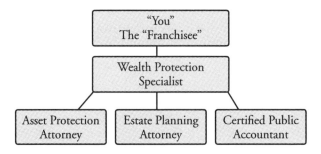

Second, you get a national support team that designs advanced strategies, oversees the local advisors, and is available to you, the client, as necessary:

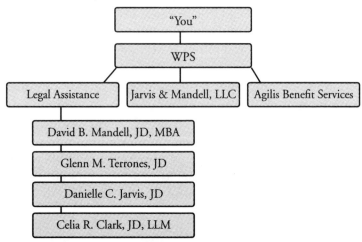

What Services are Offered Through the Wealth Protection Alliance?

Accounts Receivable Factoring

Accounts Receivable Protection

Benefits Analysis & Products

Business Overhead Expense

Buy-Sell Agreements

Buy-Sell Funding

Captive Insurance Companies

Comprehensive Estate Planning

Comprehensive Financial Planning

Deferred Compensation Planning

Disability Insurance

Dynasty Trusts

Equipment Protection

Family Limited Partnerships

Individually Managed Accounts

International LLCs

International Trusts

Investment Advisory Services

Irrevocable Trusts

Life Insurance Review

Life Insurance Sales

Life Settlements

Limited Liability Companies

Living Trusts

Long-term Care Insurance

Medical Malpractice Insurance

Mutual Funds

Non-profit Deferred Compensation

Practice Formation

Practice Restructuring

Premium Financed Insurance

Private Placement Life Insurance

Professional Employer Organization Implementation

Property & Casualty Insurance

QPRTs and other Home Protection

Real Estate Protection

Retirement Plan Analysis

Retirement Plan Implementation

Variable Annuities

Wills

529 College Saving Plans

CHAPTER THIRTEEN

Working with the Wealth Protection Alliance

Wealth Protection Planning requires multi-disciplinary expertise that one person or firm is likely unable to provide. It requires a collaborative effort from a number of specialists with the oversight of a local generalist who can quarterback the process and regularly meet with you. The local Wealth Protection Specialist can help you understand what is being done and, most importantly, make sure all of the work being done is integrated for your maximum benefit.

We have worked with a series of advisors from the Wealth Protection Alliance — a national network of top financial advisors. These advisors not only have their own successful practices in 50 cities throughout the U.S., but they have also been have been trained by us in the areas of asset protection, tax planning, and advanced business issues that specifically effect medical practices. By working with the Wealth Protection Alliance, you will have access to the expertise and experience of a number of experts in various fields through your local Wealth Protection Specialist. If you already have an attorney or accountant, he/she can be integrated into the process for maximum flexibility and convenience.

If you would like to take the first step to implementing your Wealth Protection Plan, please complete the Confidential Data Form and Asset Questionnaire in Appendix B and fax it to (888) 317-9896. A Wealth Protection Specialist will review your information and contact you to discuss you situation and how working with the Wealth Protection Alliance might benefit you. There is no cost — except 10 minutes of your time to complete and fax the form — in taking the first step to comprehensive Wealth Protection and financial freedom.

We hope you found this book helpful and we look forward to assisting you.

Contact Us Toll Free at (888) 317-9895

Fax Us Toll Free at (888) 317-9896

Appendices

Appendix A: Schedule a Seminar or Meeting

Would You Like to Meet with One of the Authors or Have an Author Address Your Group?

The authors have provided educational programs for hundreds of groups and associations, have written articles for over 250 professional publications and appeared on over 100 radio programs.

Our seminars are accredited for Continuing Professional Education credits for CPAs in all 50 states and for attorneys in a number of states. We suggest that you invite your local advisors to attend our seminars so we can make sure that any suggestions we offer may be integrated into the planning you have already done.

Typically, seminars given by the authors are scheduled three to nine months in advance. However, we are dedicated to helping our clients address their timely needs. Because we work closely with 60 offices of advanced planning specialists (The Wealth Protection Alliance) nationwide, we can often accommodate requests for seminars within 30 days.

To schedule a seminar, call (800) 554-7233 and speak to Todd or Tricia or complete the form below and fax it to us at (888) 317-9896. We will be happy to discuss particulars and negotiate an appropriate price with you. We may be able to offer continuing education credits for the attendees.

FAX to (888) 317-9896

_____ Yes, I would like to schedule a time for one of the authors or their partners to address my group or association.

_____ Yes, I would like to schedule a time to meet an author or someone in their local office.

Name: _____

Address: _____

City / State / Zip: _____

Phone: _____ Email: _____

Appendix B: Confidential Data Form

Name: _____ Birth date: _____

Spouse Name: _____ Birth date: _____

Occupation: _____ Income: _____

Spouse Occupation: _____ Income: _____

Health Status (Personal): _____

Health Status (spouse): _____

Address: _____

_____

Work Phone: _____ Fax: _____

Home Phone: _____ Cell: _____

Email: _____

# of children: _____ Ages: _____

# of grandchildren _____ Ages: _____

Years to retirement: _____

Monthly (after tax) income required during retirement: _____

What long term rate of return do you expect
to get on your retirement investments? _____

Business / Practice Information
Type of entity
(C-corp, S-corp, LLC, etc): _____ Owner / employee (circle one)

No. of owners: _____ No. of employees: _____

Gross revenue: _____ Accounts receivables: _____

Qualified plan: Yes / No (circle one)

Non-Qualified Plan: Yes / No (circle one)

Non-Real Estate Assets

Asset	Fair Market Value	Type of Funds	Basis	How is Asset Held? (own name, jointly, living trust, etc)
Pensions, Profit Sharing Plans, IRAs				Beneficiary
Brokerage Accounts, Bank Accounts, CDs				
Business Interests				
Amount of investment income earned annually				

Home and Real Estate Holdings

Property (give primary residence a *)	Fair Market Value	Amount of Mortgage	Type of Mortgage	Inception Date of Mtg.	Interest Rate	Monthly Payment (Principal)	Monthly Payment (Interest)

Life Insurance

Company Name	Insured / Policy Owner	Death Benefit	Annual Premium	Cash Value	Policy Date

Disability & Long Term Care Insurance

Company Name	Policy Owner	Type of Policy	Annual Premium	Coverage Amount

Prior Planning

Document	Y / N	Year Last Updated
Last Will & Testament		
Revocable Living Trust(s)		
Irrevocable Life Insurance Trust(s)		
Qualified Personal Residence Trust(s)		
Family Limited Partnership(s)		
Family Limited Liability Company(ies)		
Charitable Lead / Remainder Trust(s)		
Other: _____		

Concerns

Please rank each concern on a scale of 1 to 10.
(1=not concerned, 10 = very concerned):

_____ Minimizing Income Tax Liabilities

_____ Reducing Capital Gains Taxes on Investments

_____ Diversifying an Investment Portfolio

_____ Planning for Retirement

_____ Protecting Family Income against Disability/Death

_____ Protecting Wealth from Potential Lawsuits

_____ Protecting My Pension from the 83% Tax Trap

_____ Reducing Estate Taxes

_____ Planning For Parents/Elders

_____ Business Succession Planning

_____ Charitable Planning

Estate Distribution Analysis

At the time of your death, how much would you like to leave to the following
entities? Please fill out how much in dollars ($$$) and as a percentage (%),
that you would like to leave to Charity, Children, and Taxes.

Children $ _____

Children % = _____%

Charity $ _____

Charity % = _____%

Taxes $ _____

Taxes % = _____%

Professional Advisors

If we work together, we may need to coordinate the planning with your other trusted advisors. Please provide us some information about advisors you work with.

Your Accountant

Name: _____ Firm: _____

Work Phone: _____ For how long: _____

Your Attorney

Name: _____ Firm: _____

Work Phone: _____ For how long: _____

Your Investment Advisor / Financial Planner

Name: _____ Firm: _____

Work Phone: _____ For how long: _____

Appendix C: Discounted Books for Continued Education

Wealth Protection: Build and Preserve Your Financial Fortress
is the first financial and legal planning book that tailors its
recommendation to your individual situation. It is also the first book
to integrate financial, tax, legal and investment advice into a single
text. By completing a Yes/No questionnaire, you can customize the
book to fit your specific needs in the areas of Income Tax Reduction,
Investing, Asset Protection, Insurance Planning, Retirement Planning,
Estate Planning, Business Planning, and much, much more.
Regularly $24.95

Financial Secrets to Franchising Success
is the only financial and legal planning book that tailors its
recommendation to the challenges that face franchise owners and their
families. By integrating, financial, tax, legal and investment advice into
a single text, this book helps franchise owners get their hands around
the most pressing concerns — lawsuit protection, tax reduction and
business succession planning. It is a perfect compliment to *Wealth
Protection: Build and Preserve Your Financial Fortress.*
Regularly $19.95

# of Books	Item Description	Cost	Subtotal
_____	*Wealth Protection: Build & Preserve Your Financial Fortress*	$20	_____
_____	*Financial Secrets to Franchising Success*	$10	_____
	Subtotal		_____
	Shipping & Handling ($5 per book)		_____
	Total		_____

Check payable to Guardian Publishing or Credit Card

Name: _____

Address: _____

City / State / Zip: _____

Phone: (   ) _____ - _____   Email: _____

Credit Card: _____ Exp. Date ___ / ___

Signature: _____

Fax to (888) 317-9896

Appendix D: The Homestead Laws

Safeguarding Your Home by Homestead Laws

Many Americans consider their home to be their most valuable asset. In fact, you may have already thought you knew about the laws which protect your home. *Perhaps you have previously heard the term "homestead," and assumed that you could never lose your home to bad debts or other liabilities because of homestead protection. You would be wrong.* Homestead laws are hot and cold-some give you total protection, while others, are no shield whatsoever. We discovered that the best way to understand these laws and their protective power is through a series of questions and answers.

What are Homestead Laws?

Homestead laws are state statutes which protect the home from certain creditors. Forty-five states have such laws and *each state declares a certain amount of equity (value) of the homestead to be protected against particular types of creditors.* To understand whether or not these laws protect you, it is necessary to understand what the term *homestead* means.

What is a "Homestead"?

This can be very tricky, for not everything you might consider to be a "home" qualifies for "homestead" status. *Homestead exemption only applies to real estate which is your primary residence and which you own and occupy.* Beyond this, whether or not a certain piece of real estate can be considered your homestead depends completely on your state statute.

For example, many states extend homestead protection to condominiums, but some do not. Also, certain state statutes cover only single-family homes, not duplexes, triplexes, or larger structures. Some states even shield mobile homes, in the right circumstances; while others offer them no protection at all.

How Much of the Homestead's Value Do These Laws Protect?

This answer also depends on your state, but in most cases the answer is "not enough." Most states only protect between $10,000 and $60,000 of the homestead's equity. Some states, like New Jersey, provide no protection while others provide incredible protection. Given today's real estate values and the equity many people have in their home, most state homestead exemptions provide inadequate protection.

On the other hand, if you to live in Texas or Florida, your homestead is protected up to an unlimited value. In Florida or Texas, you could keep a debt-free multimillion dollar home, even when you file for bankruptcy!

Remember, *to determine how well a homestead law protects your home, compare the protected value to the equity.* First, subtract the value of any mortgages from the fair market value of your home. For example, if you live in a home with a $300,000 fair market value and a $150,000 mortgage, then your equity is $150,000. If your state protects only $20,000 through it homestead law, then you still have $130,000 equity vulnerable to lawsuits and other creditors.

Homestead Protection is not Automatic

Each state has specific requirements for claiming homestead status. In some states, you must file a declaration of homestead in a public office. Others set a time requirement for residency before homestead protection is granted. *Never assume your home is protected and do nothing because you may be wrong.* Your asset protection attorney can show you how to comply with the state law formalities.

Who Can Claim Homestead Protection?

Certain states allow only the head of household to make the homestead declaration. Others allow either spouse to do so. Beware:

if both spouses file a declaration, they could cancel each other out (in some states). Once again, have your asset protection attorney investigate who can determine who can file the declaration.

Against Whom Does the Homestead Law Protect?

While it will again depend on your state's statute, the general rule is that the homestead will protect your home from all debts (including judgments) that arise after the homestead status attached. Some states provide protection from debts incurred even before homestead status has vested.

Homestead laws won't protect your home from certain types of creditor claims. The following creditors can ignore homestead laws and take action against your home:

- The IRS and other federal agencies-if you owe federal taxes or are sued by the SEC or the EPA, you can lose your home, no matter what state you live in. If you owe state taxes, homestead may protect you, depending on the state.
- Spouses in a divorce action and family members challenging inheritances.
- Child Support claimants.
- Plaintiffs with intentional tort claims; libel, fraud, deceit, and others.
- Creditors to whom you voluntarily gave interests in your home, such as mortgages or deeds of trust.

Is There Any Downside to Making a Homestead Declaration?

Yes, there are downsides. You may have to endure legal complications if you try to sell or refinance your home after making the declaration. The bank or buyer may need you to temporarily lift the homestead exemption while the transaction closes. While this is not too burdensome, it can be inconvenient and time consuming.

The most significant downside, however, is that you will be lulled into an illusory sense of security. For example, today you may have $30,000 worth of equity in your home. If you live in a state with a $30,000 homestead exemption, your home is fully protected today. But is it protected in the future? Lulled into a false sense of security, you believe your house is still fully protected. Yet, as the years move on, you accumulate more equity in your home. If you are eventually sued 5, 7, 10 years down the road, all the additional equity you have built in your home could be lost. *Asset protection clients never suffer this mistake. Their advisors analyze how homestead protects them now, and how it will continue to do so in the future by using other tools to protect their savings wherever homestead proves inadequate.*

Three Ways to Maximize Homestead Protection

Your asset protection lawyer should not have you file a homestead declaration until he/she has considered all of your financial circumstances. The goal is to determine whether homestead protection can be the strongest "building block" of your financial fortress. To maximize homestead protection:

- The spouse who is more vulnerable to lawsuits should file the declaration, so the protection can shield against claims facing that spouse.

- If you have multiple homes, file the homestead declaration for the home with the most equity exposed. This can be tricky because the person declaring homestead must show that he lives at that dwelling with the intent to make it his permanent domicile. If your homestead status is challenged, be prepared to answer the following:

  - Where you filed your federal tax returns
  - Where your mail is received
  - Where you are registered to vote
  - Where you spend most of your time.

- Move to a state where the homestead exemption is unlimited — like Florida or Texas. This is part of the more general asset protection tactic: convert wealth held in non-exempt assets into wealth held in exempt assets.

Appendix E: Wage Protection

Creditors who win a judgment against you can seize your paycheck through a *wage garnishment*. A creditor's right to take your paycheck is limited. Both federal and state laws partially protect wages.

Like the homestead laws, each state's protection for wages differs. Texas and Florida are again the most favorable to debtors and exempt 100% of wages from creditor garnishment. The remaining states protect a certain percentage of one's wages and allow the creditor to take the rest.

Even if your state offers only limited protection of your wages, the federal *Consumer Credit Protection Act (CCPA)* sets a limit on the amount a creditor can take from your wages. Because it is a federal law, the CCPA trumps any state law which offers less wage protection. Thus, if your wages are threatened by a creditor, you will be protected at least by the limits of CCPA and possibly more, depending on your state's law. The CCPA limits the amount of wages a creditor can take to the lesser of:

- 25% of your disposable income per week *(disposable income* means your paycheck after federal and state withholding taxes have been taken out), or

- The amount by which your weekly disposable income for the week exceeds 30 times the federal minimum hourly wage then in effect.

Appendix F: Protection for Life Insurance & Annuities

Life Insurance Can Protect You In Many Ways

Life insurance, like a home, is protected solely by state law. Today, all 50 states have laws protecting life insurance, but they all protect differing amounts. Some general trends:

- Most states shield the entire policy proceeds from the creditors of the Policyholder. Some also protect against the beneficiaries' creditors.

- States which do not protect the entire policy proceeds set amounts above which the creditor can take proceeds. For example, Arizona exempts the first $20,000 of proceeds.

- Many states protect the policy proceeds only if the policy beneficiaries are the policyholder's spouse, children, or other dependents.

- Most states also exempt proceeds from term and group life policies.

- Some states protect a policy's cash surrender value in addition to the policy proceeds. If you have substantial cash value in a life insurance policy(ies), be sure to examine your state exemptions to determine how well protected you are.

- No state can protect life insurance from the IRS—they can take your insurance proceeds and cash value. If you already have an IRS problem or anticipate owing more taxes than you can pay, you may want to consider an Irrevocable Life Insurance Trust.

- If the policy is purchased as part of a fraudulent transfer, a court can undo the policy, like any other fraudulent transfer.

Maximizing Life Insurance Protection

An important part of any asset protection plan is the irrevocable life insurance trust. If the beneficiaries have creditor concerns, the policy has cash value, the IRS is a potential creditor, or if you live in a state with minimal protection, such a trust is essential. A properly drafted irrevocable life insurance trust provides maximum protection for your policy proceeds and its cash value — shielding them entirely from all creditors of the policyholder and the beneficiaries, including the IRS. It also may provide significant tax benefits.

TIP: Never assign your life insurance policy to a bank or other creditor. Even if your policy was originally exempt, you could lose the exemption if you made such an assignment.

Annuities — An Asset — Protected Investment in Many States

An annuity is a investment contract where the investor pays a certain amount of money up front, and the seller then pays the investor back at a certain interest rate in fixed installments. Most states do not protect annuities from creditor claims. However, in the states that do exempt annuities, annuities are an ideal tool to safeguard wealth. Depending on the state exemption, there may be a limit on the value of the annuities to be protected.

As part of asset protection planning, also review your investment objectives. By investing in life insurance and annuities, you may achieve both your investment goals and asset protection.

Appendix G: Retirement Plans

Retirement Plans: A Mixed Bag of Protection

Along with the family home, an individual's retirement savings is often the most important asset he owns. In terms of asset protection, retirement plans must be divided into: 1) ERISA-qualified pension plans and 2) all other retirement plans, such as *Individual Retirement Accounts (IRAs)* and Keogh plans.

ERISA-Qualified Pension Plans

ERISA-qualified means the pension meets the requirements of the *Employee Retirement Income Security Act of 1974 (ERISA)*. ERISA was enacted specifically to protect the rights of employees enrolled in benefit plans sponsored by their employers or unions. A key requirement of ERISA is that the pension plan must be a "spendthrift trust" — one that prohibits the beneficiary from in any way assigning the plan's principal or income.

A 1992 U.S. Supreme Court decision solidified the protection for ERISA-qualified pension plans. *The Court clearly concluded that ERISA-qualified plans cannot be taken by creditors, whether in bankruptcy, by lawsuit, or through other means.* This decision applies to all ERISA-qualified pension plans. Public pensions (those funded by state or federal government) have always been exempt from creditor claims.

Is your pension ERISA-qualified? The answer is by no means clear and there are seemingly different standards for civil courts and bankruptcy courts. Nevertheless, here are a few guiding principals: Firstly, if both the owners and employees are covered by the plan, it is highly likely to be considered ERISA-qualified. Secondly, if you are a small business — perhaps just two or three partners or family owned *with no employees participating in the plan* — recent trends in the law indicate that the plan is more likely to be considered ERISA-qualified if the entity funding the plan is operating as a "C" Corporation. General partnerships and sole proprietorships are afforded little or no protection in this regard. It is unclear how

Limited Liability Companies, subchapter "S" Corporations and Professional Corporations will fare in this regard but a simple "rule of thumb" might be stated this way: the more your entity behaves like a "C" Corporation, the more likely it is that your plan will be deemed ERISA-qualified. Again, much depends on the laws in your jurisdiction and it is strongly urged that one contact an asset protection lawyer to review the pension documents themselves.

Keogh Plans

If you participate in a Keogh plan that has multiple participants, the same principles that apply to ERISA-qualified pensions will apply to your Keogh plan. Most likely, the plan will be safe, whether attacked by one creditor in a lawsuit or a host of creditors in a bankruptcy. A sole-participant Keogh plan, however, is considerably more vulnerable and will most likely be treated like an IRA from a creditor protection standpoint.

State courts routinely allow creditors to seize sole-participant Keogh funds, on the theory that the beneficiary/debtor is able to withdraw the funds at will; and, because the beneficiary/debtor is his own trustee.

IRA's

IRAs are less secure than ERISA-qualified plans and Keoghs. An IRA is basically a custodial account set aside for the owner, who can withdraw the funds at any time. As there is no "spendthrift" provision and no trustee, there is no federal protection for IRAs. Also, because the owner can always reach the IRA funds by incurring a tax penalty, courts have held that creditors should have the same right to get at the funds. Nevertheless, many states exempt all retirement funds, including IRAs, from creditors.

Because protection of IRAs can only come from the states, federal government creditors like the IRS, the EPA, or the SEC can take your IRA. Although it is often last on their list of assets to seize, the

IRS can and will eventually take your IRA funds if you owe back taxes.

TIP: If you need last-second asset protection because a creditor is about to seize assets, it may make sense to liquidate your IRA and transfer the funds into an exempt asset, or to pay other debts. While you will incur an early withdrawal penalty, that is preferable to losing the entire amount to a creditor seizure.

Appendix H: Before You Buy or Sell a Franchise

When Chris and David were in business school at UCLA, they had a professor name Bill Cockrum. Bill had served on the board of one the nation's most prestigious investment firms in the world. Despite his impeccable credentials, Chris and David thought him to be a fool when he stated on the first day of *Finance 231 — Entrepreneurial Finance* that he would teach us that:

**it is more important to name the terms of a deal
than it is to name the price of a deal.**

Your reaction to this statement is probably the same as ours was. However, when you look deeper into the transaction of buying or selling any business, you will see that there is a lot of truth to Professor Cockrum's statement. Consider the following points:

1. Buyers want to buy assets. They do not want to buy stock. This is because buyers of stock assume all liabilities from the previous business. If you buy a business through a stock sale and a lawsuit arises after you purchase the business (from an event that took place before your purchase of the business) you are legally responsible for the loss.

2. Sellers do not want to sell assets. They want to sell stock. In most businesses, the goodwill is significant value of the business. Though a stock sale and asset sale can be taxed as capital gains, the goodwill is taxed at ordinary income tax rates. This creates a conflict of interest between the Buyer and Seller.

3. Buyers want Sellers to sign noncompete agreements and Sellers don't want to sign noncompete agreements.

4. Buyers like to pay for the sale with deferred salary. This is fully deductible to the buyer and fully taxable at ordinary income tax rates to the Seller. Sellers obviously prefer capital gains tax treatment over ordinary income tax treatment

since the highest federal long term capital gains tax rate is currently 15% and the highest marginal federal tax rate on ordinary income is 35%.

5. Buyers don't care about the Seller's estate planning and the Seller obviously does.

The key point to make in this Appendix is that the details of the sale are very important. If you only worry about the "price" of the sale, you could end up paying almost 50% of the sale price in taxes, subject your family to unnecessary lawsuit risk, and create a substantial amount of unnecessary estate taxes for your heirs. If you work with a savvy investment banker and a team of advisors who understand tax and asset protection, you can structure a purchase or sale that fits into YOUR overall Wealth Protection Plan. One of the founders of the WPA, Dale Edwards, has years of investment banking experience. Your local WPA office can arrange to have Mr. Edwards and the local team of attorneys and CPAs available to help you with the legal and tax questions surrounding your potential sale or purchase. Please call (800) 554-7233 to speak with the local WPA member in your area.

Appendix I: Members of the Wealth Protection Alliance

As you learned in Chapters 12 and 13, the Wealth Protection Alliance has offices in over 50 cities across the country. In addition, the WPA's Preferred Professional Program has over 100 law firms and accounting firms who are experienced in the areas of tax, asset protection and estate planning.

Without the help of our partners across the country, we would not be able to bring such comprehensive high-level planning to business owners like you. Special thanks go out to these valuable members of our team. The partial list of our members includes:

Dale Edwards, David Wright, Jenny Piper and the staff of Agilis Benefits Services, Pramod Ahuja, Bob Baker, Chuck Baldwin, Barbara Barton, John Baxa, George Becknell, Todd Bramson, David "Mike" Breedlove, Brian Breuel, James Broussard, Chris Broyles, Phil Calhoun, Don Camphausen, John Cane, Gregory Carroll, Bryan Church, Steve Church, Tom Clark, Chuck Cleveland, Frank Cochran, Ryan Coker, Thomas Collins, Michael Coulson, Rob Davenport, Tim Dempsey, Peter DiCaro, Richard DiPasquale, Nancy Dreyer, Steve Dunbar, Steven Dunn, John Ellard, Chris Fay, Neil Finestone, Rao Garuda, Bob Gutherman, Michael Halloran, Jeff Hamblen, Jim Harris, Todd Harris, Bill Hartman, Peter Hartman, J. Thomas Hassell, John "David" Hebert, David House, Russell Jacobs III, Jeffrey Jaskol, J. Michael Jensen, Fred Johnson, Chris Jordan, Jordan Katz, John Kelly, Sean King, Thomas King, Chuck Kissee, Paul Klass, Charlie Kuhn, William Lloyd, Russell Lo, Peggy Lombardo, Armond Madirossians, Hugh McDonald, Keith Mohn, William Muench, Jeff Nesseth, Jason O'Dell, Kevin Perlberg, Gerald "Skip" Raymond, Bob Rever, Greg Rever, Steve Rivetti, Charles Russo, Dennis Sanchez, Ali Sayas, Steve Scammell, Lou Shapiro, Shaker Sherif, Mark Smallhouse, John Steiger, Ernie Stiba, Sandy Stokes, Scott Syphers, Vance Syphers, Maureen Verduyn, Frank Wong, and Rob Young.